Anonymous

Hood's Cook Book

Anonymous

Hood's Cook Book

ISBN/EAN: 9783744789172

Printed in Europe, USA, Canada, Australia, Japan

Cover: Foto ©Lupo / pixelio.de

More available books at **www.hansebooks.com**

COOK BOOK.

These receipts include those published in Mrs. Mayor Stott's famous "Practical Cook Book," she having kindly allowed us to use them. Other valuable ones have been added, together with much useful matter. The *blank pages* and *index* will commend themselves to every one, as new receipts can be added and all be easily found, thus making HOOD'S COOK BOOK the most desirable one that has ever been given away. Given to every housekeeper on application at our store, or sent on receipt of address.

COMPLIMENTS OF

C. I. HOOD & CO., Apothecaries,

The Object of Hood's Cook Book.

In the publishing of this book we desire to accomplish two things. First, to put into the hands of housekeepers receipts of such value that they will be in constant use. Second, to place in every family the unquestionable proof of the real value of Hood's Sarsaparilla. It will be noticed that this proof comes from the worthiest citizens in our immediate vicinity. Any one wishing to confer with them in regard to the wonderful effects of Hood's Sarsaparilla, can do so.

SCROFULOUS HUMORS of the worst possible types, whose cure by Hood's Sarsaparilla seem hardly less than miracles, will be found on pages 9, 13, 16, 23, 38, 60. Some other cures noted are—

SALT RHEUM, page 48, 59.
APPETITE SHARPENED, pages 16, 25.
LOSS OF FLESH, page 25.
DEBILITY, pages 9, 25, 41, 44.
INDIGESTION, page 44.
SORE NOSE, page 44.
SORE ON THE LEG, page 54.
CANCEROUS HUMOR, page 58.
SCROFULOUS BUNCH IN THE NECK, page 38.

If your family druggist does not keep Hood's Sarsaparilla, he will gladly get it for you; if not we will send it to you on receipt of price. We guarantee satisfaction every time, and our agents are authorized to do the same.

Very truly, your obt. servants,

C. I. HOOD & CO.,

Lowell, Mass.

RECEIPTS.

SOUPS.

Of all the operations of cookery, none is more important, nor usually more negligently executed, than the preparation of soups. Setting aside the consideration of economy, to begin dinner with a light soup is decidedly wholesome, and serves to divert the danger of eating too heavily of solid meat; for it is an error for any one to fancy that when he has eaten heartily of roast beef only, he has necessarily made a wholesome dinner.

The richest soups are made by boiling several kinds of meat together, as beef, mutton and veal.

Hood's Tooth Powder whitens the teeth.

BEEF SOUP STOCK.

Take a shank of beef and cut the meat in fine pieces; take out the marrow and with a piece of butter put into a kettle, put over the fire and when hot add the meat and cook till brown, then add the bones and sufficient hot water to cover, boil four hours, strain and set away to cool.

BEEF SOUP.

Take sufficient soup stock, boil onion, carrot, potatoes and vegetables to suit taste, in a little water, and strain into the soup stock; add pepper, salt, etc., to suit.

TOMATO SOUP.

Put three pints of tomatoes, stewed, strained and sweetened, to two quarts of beef stock, add an onion, salt and pepper.

PEA SOUP.

Take a pint of split peas, and when carefully picked over and washed, put them into a pint of water, soak in morning, three hours before dinner put them into a pot with a quart more water and about half a pound of pork (less if you wish the soup not very rich), boil it steadily and be careful to stir it often lest it should burn. It may need more water before dinner and can be made of whatever thickness you prefer. If you prefer to have the soup without pork, use the liquor in which the beef or other fresh meat has been boiled instead of water and use no pork.

YEAST, No. 1.

One and a half cups of raw grated potatoes, one cup of white sugar, two-thirds of a cup of salt, pour on four quarts of boiling water, stir while pouring in. Steep a handful of hops and stir in the yeast; when cold add one and a half cups of yeast.

Hood's Tooth Powder hardens the gums.

YEAST, No. 2.

Take six good-sized potatoes, wash and pare them and put to boil in two quarts of water, and with them a small handful of hops in a small bag tightly tied. When the potatoes are quite soft take them out and mash them fine, pouring upon them the water in which they were boiled, adding a little water to make up for what they have boiled away; half a cup of salt and the same quantity of sugar. When cooled to a lukewarm temperature add one cup of yeast to ferment it. Keep in a cool place.

BROWN BREAD, No. 1.

One quart of meal, two-thirds of it rye, one-third Indian, a cup of molasses, a teaspoonful of salt. Mix it very soft with a pint and a half of sour milk, in which is dissolved a teaspoonful of saleratus. Boil three and a half hours.

Hood's Sarsaparilla purifies the blood.

BROWN BREAD, No. 2.

One pint of sour milk, two teacups of molasses, three cups corn meal, one and a half cups of flour, one-half teaspoonful of salt, two teaspoonfuls of soda. Steam three hours.

BROWN BREAD, No. 3.

One and a half pints of sweet milk, one coffee cup of molasses, stir in a thin batter of one-half Indian meal and one-half Graham, one small teaspoonful of soda. Steam it two hours with the cover on, one hour uncovered.

Hood's Sarsaparilla restores and renovates the whole system.

Erysipelas or Salt-Rheum.

MESSRS. C. I. HOOD & CO. Lowell, June 20, 1878.

DEAR SIRS—Allow me to tell you my story for the benefit of others. My mother and sister have been troubled with the Salt-Rheum a good many years. I never had a blotch on *my* face until May, 1876, when three hard purple bunches came on my chin, the size of the end of my finger. One doctor told me it was Salt-Rheum, another Erysipelas, while a third said it was caused by eating fruit. These physicians gave me medicine, but none of it did me any good. This ran along till the following January, when it got so bad I was ashamed to go out. My nurse finally persuaded me to try HOOD'S SARSAPARILLA. Although the first bottle made me feel sick, still I had confidence in it and persisted in taking it. This sick feeling was undoubtedly caused by my being very bilious. When I had taken about half of the second bottle I began to feel decidedly better, and after this my chin seemed to improve every day. When I had finished the second bottle I felt like a new person; my appetite had been very poor, but has been splendid ever since. I tell my friends I *can do two days' work in one* now.

Some of my friends told me they did not think it was going to do me any good, and I must admit I was discouraged a good many times, for I had faithfully tried so many things without receiving any permanent good; still I hung on, and HOOD'S SARSAPARILLA has fixed my chin almost as good as new, and I am only too happy to testify to its value. I used one box of your Olive Ointment—you don't praise it half enough. With much gratitude, I am very truly yours. MRS. A. D. ALLEN, South Street, Lowell.

(At Mr. John Nichols's.) Read pages 48 and 59.

The letter which follows adds another to the long list of grateful ones who are to-day doing their utmost to extend the knowledge of this wonderful remedy among their friends.

CANKER AND DIPHTHERIA.

Winchester, Mass., Sept. 27, 1878.

MESSRS. C. I. HOOD & Co., Lowell, Mass. *Dear Sirs*—Will you please send me two more bottles of your SARSAPARILLA? I enclose postal order for $2. My little boy had the Diphtheria a few years ago, and has had trouble with humor and abscesses ever since; have not had anything do him any good until I tried your SARSAPARILLA. He is beginning to get better, and I think one more bottle will cure him. As for myself I feel that I cannot recommend HOOD'S SARSAPARILLA too highly, for I have been troubled with Canker now for a number of years, and I can begin to see that your medicine is curing me. I do not feel that I can be without it, so please send as soon as possible. MRS. E. F. METCALF.

Hood's Sarsaparilla is sold by all Druggists.
$1.00 a bottle, or six large bottles for $5.00. Trial size 50 cts.

C. I. HOOD & CO., Apothecaries, Lowell, Mass.

Hood's Tooth Powder preserves the teeth.

MRS. II.'S BREAD.

Sift eight quarts of flour into the kneading tray, put in a pint of yeast, mixed with a pint of lukewarm water, and work up this with surrounding flour till it makes a thick batter. Then scatter a handful of flour over the batter, lay a warm cloth over the whole, and set in a warm place. This is called sponge. When the sponge is risen so as to make cracks in the flour over it, scatter over it two table-spoonfuls of salt, and put in two quarts of wetting, warm but not hot enough to scald the yeast. Knead the whole thoroughly for as much as half an hour, form into a round mass, scatter a little flour over it, cover it, set it to rise in a warm place. In winter it is best to put the bread to rise over night, keeping it warm, in summer in the morning.

ANOTHER BREAD.

Five quarts of flour, piece of butter size of an egg worked in, one large spoonful of sugar, one small spoonful of salt, one quart of water or milk, two-thirds of a cup of yeast, let it rise over night, knead thoroughly in the morning and let it rise again in the bread tins. Bake an hour and a quarter in a moderate oven.

Hood's Sarsaparilla restores the whole system.

THIRD BREAD.

One quart bolted Indian meal, scalded with boiling water; when cool add one cup of yeast, one quart of flour, one quart rye meal, two or three spoonfuls of molasses, a little salt; mix with lukewarm water. Mould with the hand and put to rise over night; in the morning add one-half teaspoonful of soda. Bake in biscuit or in loaves.

RYE CAKES.

One pint scalding hot milk, one-half cup Indian meal, one-half cup sugar, one cup rye meal, two cups of flour; cool and then add a little salt, and one-half cup of yeast. Let this rise over night. In the morning add one-half teaspoonful of saleratus and two eggs.

BREAKFAST CAKE.

One cup of sugar, two cups of milk, two-thirds of a cup of melted butter, three eggs, one quart of flour, two teaspoonfuls of cream tartar, one teaspoonful of soda. Bake twenty minutes.

MUFFINS, No. 1.

One quart of milk, one egg, one spoonful of butter, two spoonfuls of lard, one-half cup of yeast, and flour enough to make a batter a little thicker than griddle cakes. Put to rise over night.

MUFFINS, No. 2.

One pint of new milk, four eggs, one teaspoonful of salt, flour enough for a batter.

CORN CAKE, No. 1.

Two cups of white Indian meal, one cup of flour, one pint of water, one egg, two-thirds cup of sugar, two teaspoonfuls cream tartar, one teaspoonful of soda, a small piece of butter and a little salt.

Hood's Tooth Powder preserves and beautifies the teeth.

JENNIE LUNGES.

Half a cup of melted butter, two tablespoonfuls of sugar, one cup of sweet milk, two teaspoonfuls of cream tartar, one teaspoonful soda, two eggs, three cups flour, and a little salt. Bake in small cups twenty minutes.

PARKER HOUSE ROLLS.

One quart of cold boiled milk, two quarts of flour, one large tablespoonful of lard rubbed into the flour; make a hole in the middle of the flour; take one full cup of yeast, one-half cup of sugar, add the milk and pour into the flour with a little salt; let it stand as it is until morning, then knead it hard and let it rise; knead again at four in the afternoon; cut out ready to bake and let it rise again. Bake twenty minutes.

Hereditary Scrofula.

Are you aware that in your blood the taint of Scrofula has a prominent place? This is true of every one. It is liable at any time, on the slightest provocation, to develop itself in some insidious disease. Consumption and many other diseases are outgrowths of this impurity of the blood.

While a single bottle of HOOD'S SARSAPARILLA has repeatedly effected wonderful cures, it is hardly reasonable that one should expect to be cured in a short time of a disease that may have covered months and years. All we ask is a fair trial, and we beg those who are suffering to extend to Hood's Sarsaparilla one-tenth the patience they have exercised in enduring the misery inflicted by their disease, and a small fraction of persistency like that with which the disease has clung to them. Relief has followed this course in every instance from which we have heard.

37 SCROFULOUS SORES CURED.

MESSRS. C. I. HOOD & CO.: Gentlemen—In November last an itching sensation under my arms resulted in two abscesses. One of these extended up on my shoulder and became a very deep running sore, larger than the palm of my hand. In February folowing a bunch grew on my knee as big as my fist. I had it lanced in April. This also became a running sore. No one can know how much I suffered. At this time I had thirty-seven sores—one on my head almost as large as the palm of my hand. Dr. —— of Westford feared this would affect my brain, as it was a very ugly thing. I was living in Manchester, N. H., at the time these sores came. My physician, Dr. ——, wrote my mother that I could not possibly get well, and although he thought I would die on the way, he advised her to take me home. I reached Westford and was put under medical treatment, but kept failing.

When I began to take HOOD'S SARSAPARILLA (eight months ago) these sores had completely prostrated me. I was confined to my bed, and no one thought it possible for me to get well. My very life was exhausted; I had no appetite, and the only thing I could eat was a little cracker and water. Anything else seemed to choke me. The doctor gave me everything he could think of to give me an appetite, but without success, and at last told mother he didn't know of anything more he could do for me. One day mother read one of your circulars to me about HOOD'S SARSAPARILLA. I said to her, "I want some of that medicine." And I am glad to tell you that in eight days after I began to take it, my appetite came to me and has been good ever since. My sores are nearly all healed; I am almost as strong and well as before I had this awful time, and now I am going to do my own work. I cannot over-express my gratitude, because I cannot help feeling that HOOD'S SARSAPARILLA has saved my life. I know four persons who are now taking the Sarsaparilla, and it's doing them all good. I know it is a wonderful medicine. Very truly yours,

MRS. LIZZIE J. COLE,
Westford. Mass.

[Now living in Windham, N. H.; daughter of Mrs. Isaac Green, of Westford.]

C. I. HOOD & CO., Apothecaries, Lowell, Mass.

Hood's Tooth Powder sweetens the breath.

BUCKWHEAT CAKES

One quart buckwheat flour, one teaspoonful of salt, stir in water to make a thin batter; beat thoroughly four table-spoonfuls home-brewed yeast. Set the batter in a warm place; let it rise over night; add one teaspoonful of soda in the morning.

JOKERS.

Two cups Graham meal, one cup of flour, a little salt, two eggs, well beaten, added after flour and milk are mixed to a batter thick as pound cake. Bake in a quick oven.

GRAHAM ROLLS, No. 1.

Two cups Graham meal, one-half cup of flour, one egg, two teaspoonfuls of cream tartar, one teaspoonful of soda, one-half cup of sugar and a little salt.

Hood's Sarsaparilla eradicates scrofula.

GRAHAM ROLLS, No. 2.

One quart Graham flour, 1 cup sugar, 1 cup yeast, 1 table-spoonful butter rubbed in the flour; mix as hard as you can stir with a spoon, let it rise over night and bake in roll pans; do not sift the flour.

ROLLS.

Take two quarts of flour and work in a large spoonful of lard; half a pint of milk boiled and cooled, add it to the flour and work thoroughly; add one-half cup of yeast and a little sugar. If for breakfast mix at noon and let rise until bedtime, then roll out and lay on the cake board until time to bake for breakfast. If for tea mix at night and roll in the morning. Bake fifteen or twenty minutes.

NEWPORT CAKES.

Two cups of milk, three eggs, one great spoonful of sugar, one of butter, one teaspoonful of cream tartar, one-half teaspoonful of soda. Make a thin batter.

Hood's Sarsaparilla makes the weak strong.

JENNIE'S SALLIE LUND GEMS.

One egg, two tablespoonfuls of melted butter, one cup of sweet milk, two tablespoonfuls sugar, two cups flour, one teaspoonful cream tartar, one-half teaspoonful saleratus. Bake fifteen minutes.

JENNY LIND DROP CAKES.

Two and a half cups of flour, a small piece of butter, one cup of sweet milk, one-half cup of sugar, one tablespoonful of cream tartar, one-half teaspoonful of soda, a little salt, one egg broken in after the rest is put together.

Hood's Tooth Powder sweetens the breath.

OATMEAL CAKES.

One cup of cream, two cups of sour milk, two tablespoonfuls of sugar, one large teaspoonful of soda, oatmeal sufficient to make a thick batter.

RYE BREAKFAST CAKES.

Two cups of rye meal, one-half cup molasses, a little salt, a cup and a half of sweet milk to mix it very soft, and one teaspoonful of saleratus. Bake at once in a roll pan or muffin rings.

COCOANUT CAKE, No. 1.

Two well-beaten eggs, two tablespoonfuls of butter, two cups prepared cocoanut, one cup sugar, one-half cup of milk, one teaspoonful cream tartar, one-half teaspoonful soda; soak the cocoanut in milk.

COCOANUT CAKE, No. 2.

Three-fourths of a pound of flour, half a pound of butter, mixed together; one pound of sugar and the yolks of five eggs mixed together; mix these with one large cocoanut; beat the whites of the eggs to a froth, and put in half a teaspoonful of soda and one of cream tartar. This is sufficient for two loaves.

Hood's Sarsaparilla cures indigestion.

GEMS.

Two cups of flour, one cup of milk, one cup water, a little salt, mix well and pour into iron-clad pans that have been heated very hot indeed, first putting a piece of butter in each partition. Bake quickly in a very hot oven.

Hood's Tooth Powder is only 25 cents a bottle.

APPLE FRITTERS.

Quarter and slice your apples, make a batter of two eggs, one cup of milk, a little salt and flour, or the same as for fried oysters; put in your apples and fry in hot fat the same as oysters. Very nice for breakfast.

POP-OVERS.

Three cups of milk, three cups of flour, three eggs. Bake half an hour in a quick oven in cups.

MARY ANN'S CREAM CAKE.

One pint of water, one pint of flour, one-half pint of butter; when the water boils put in the butter to melt, and stir in the flour. Set away to cool and then mix in seven eggs. Drop in a tin and bake in a quick oven. Cream for same—one pint of milk, four eggs, two cups of sugar, one cup of flour; beat sugar, eggs and flour together and stir in the milk while boiling. Flavor to taste.

PLAIN DARK CAKE.

One and one-half cups of sugar, two spoonfuls of molasses, one cup butter, one-half cup sour milk, one spoonful of soda, two eggs, two and one-half cups of flour, a little of all kinds of spice, currants and raisins.

GOLD CAKE.

Two cups not quite full of flour, the yolks of four eggs, one cup of sugar, one-half cup of butter, one-half cup of sweet milk, one-half teaspoonful of soda, one teaspoonful cream tartar. Flavor to taste.

Hood's Sarsaparilla is delicate to take.

Spring Medicine.

What will convince you of the wonderful curative properties combined in HOOD'S SARSAPARILLA, if the remarkable cures that have been effected by its use fail to impress upon your mind this repeatedly proven fact? Thousands are using it, and all declare that it is a medicine possessing all and even more than we claim for it. My friend, if you are sick or in that condition that you cannot call yourself either sick or well, go and get a bottle of HOOD'S SARSAPARILLA and realize yourself how this medicine hits the right spot, and puts all the machinery of your body into working order.

One of our prominent business men said to us the other day:— "In the spring my wife got all run down and could not eat anything; passing your store I saw a pile of HOOD'S SARSAPARILLA in the window, and I got a bottle. After she had been taking it a week she had a rousing appetite, and it did her everything. She took three bottles, and it was the best three dollars I ever invested."

The following testimonial from a reliable gentleman, who has especially observed the effects resulting from the use of more than fifty bottles of HOOD'S SARSAPARILLA by different persons, is only one of many at our disposal, and proves the following to be a fact, namely: that HOOD'S SARSAPARILLA is superior to all other preparations as a specific remedy for Scrofula and the numerous diseases springing from this taint in the blood, the extent of which must be realized, when statistics show that a large majority of our population are suffering from its influence, either directly or indirectly.

WILTON, N. H., Jan. 15th, 1876.

MESSRS. C. I. HOOD & Co., Lowell, Mass.

GENTS: The little girl for whom I procured your Sarsaparilla was so badly afflicted with Scrofula that the side of her neck, extending all over the ear and up into the hair, was one complete mass of matter. At this stage of the eruption I gave her a part of a bottle of Hood's Sarsaparilla, and before she had taken all of that it began to heal. I then got one bottle more and that cured her completely, leaving no scar to show that she had ever been troubled by that terrible disease, Scrofula. The beneficial effect derived from the use of Hood's Sarsaparilla by those for whom I have procured it, has in every instance been more speedy and positive than I have ever found to be the case from the use of any other preparation of the kind. Very truly yours,

E. G. WOODMAN.

Hood's Sarsaparilla is sold by all Druggists.
$1.00 a bottle, or six large bottles for $5.00. Trial size, 50 cts.

C. I. HOOD & CO., Apothecaries, Lowell, Mass.

Hood's Tooth Powder preserves the teeth.

14

SILVER CAKE.

Two cups of flour, the whites of four eggs, one cup of sugar, one-half cup of sweet milk, one teaspoonful cream tartar, one-half teaspoonful of soda. Flavor to taste.

Hood's Sarsaparilla cleanses the blood of humors.

ANNIE'S CHOCOLATE CAKE.

One full cup of butter, two cups of flour, two cups of sugar, one cup—not quite full—milk, one-half teaspoonful of soda, one teaspoonful cream tartar, five eggs, leaving out the whites of two; rub butter and sugar together, add eggs, two-thirds of the milk, then flour, then the rest of the milk in which you have dissolved the soda; while hot, spread with an icing made of the whites of eggs, one and a half cups of pulverized sugar, two teaspoonfuls essence vanilla and six tablespoonfuls of vanilla chocolate.

MARBLE CAKE.

For the white cake—one cup of butter, three cups of white sugar, five cups of flour, even full, one-half cup of sweet milk, one-half teaspoonful of soda, whites of eight eggs; flavor with lemon. For the dark cake—one cup of butter, two cups brown sugar, one cup of molasses, one cup of sour milk, one teaspoonful of soda, four cups of flour, yolks of eight eggs and one whole egg, spices of all sorts; put in pans, first a layer of dark, then a layer of white, and so on, finishing with a dark layer. Bake in a hot oven.

WHITE MOUNTAIN CAKE, No. 1.

Three cups of sugar, one cup of milk, two cups of butter, four eggs, six cups of flour, two teaspoonfuls cream tartar, one teaspoonful of soda; flavor with lemon.

WHITE MOUNTAIN CAKE, No. 2.

Three eggs, one cup of sugar, one-half cup of milk, one-half cup of butter, two cups of flour, one teaspoonful of soda, two teaspoonfuls cream tartar; flavor to taste.

ANOTHER CHOCOLATE CAKE.

Two cups of sugar, one cup of butter, one cup of sweet milk, three and a half cups of flour, three whole eggs and the yolks of two more, one teaspoonful of cream tartar, one-half teaspoonful of soda. Frosting for same—whites of two eggs beaten with sugar quite stiff, three table-spoonfuls grated chocolate, teaspoonful of vanilla.

Hood's Tooth Powder contains nothing injurious.

HERMIT CAKES.

One-half cup of butter, one and a half cups of sugar, three eggs, one teaspoonful of all kinds of spice, one-half teaspoonful of soda dissolved in a little water; mix up stiff and roll.

LILY CAKE.

Two cups of sugar, one cup of butter, mixed together; one cup of sweet milk, one-half teaspoonful of soda, one cup of corn starch, two cups of flour, one teaspoonful of cream tartar, whites of five eggs. Flavor, and frost with chocolate frosting.

QUEEN'S CAKE.

One and three-quarters pounds flour, one and a half pounds of sugar, three-quarters of a pound of butter, six eggs, one pint of milk, one pound of raisins, one glass of brandy, one nutmeg, one teaspoonful soda dissolved in the milk.

DANBURY, OR GOLD AND SILVER CAKE.

Gold cake—three cups of sugar, one cup of butter, five cups of flour, one and a half cups of sweet milk, one teaspoonful of cream tartar, half a teaspoonful of soda, the yolks of twelve eggs. Flavor with vanilla. Silver cake—Whites of twelve eggs, three cups of sugar, one cup of butter, one cup of sweet milk, one teaspoonful of cream tartar, one-half teaspoonful of soda. Flavor with almond. Five cups of flour.

That Extreme Tired Feeling.

" The first bottle has done my daughter a great deal of good; her food does not distress her now nor does she suffer from *that extreme tired feeling* which she did before taking HOOD'S SARSAPARILLA."

Other Blood Purifiers ruin the appetite. HOOD'S SARSAPARILLA stimulates and sharpens it.

A Severe Case of Scrofulous Humor Cured.

Lowell. Mass., May 15, 1877.

Messrs. C. I. HOOD & Co. Gentlemen — Allow me to tell you how very valuable your Sarsaparilla has proved itself in my family. My youngest son has always been troubled with Scrofulous Humor, sores in his head discharging from his ears, a running sore on the back of his ear for two years. his eyelids would fester and ulcerate, discharging so that I was obliged to wash them open every morning. his eyelashes nearly all coming out; he was exceedingly dainty, most of the time eating but two slight meals a day. We were unable to find anything that had the least effect upon him till last spring (1876) we gave him two bottles of HOOD'S SARSAPARILLA. His appetite improved at once, and it was a real pleasure to see him eat with the keen relish of a little pig. The back of his ear healed up without a scar, and not a sore in his head since. "Truth is stranger than fiction." The above are facts, and you are at liberty to use them as you please. Sincerely yours,

MRS. N. C. SANBORN.
108 East Merrimack St.

HOOD'S SARSAPARILLA strengthens and builds up the system while it eradicates disease.

A young lady tells us. " HOOD'S SARSAPARILLA is doing wonders. I haven't felt so well before for six months." Hundreds have reported the same and are telling it to their friends, who in turn get a bottle. try it, and so it keeps repeating itself. *A thing possessing real merit, as Hood's Sarsaparilla undoubtedly does, is bound to meet general use. Satisfaction guaranteed every time. We mean this!*

Appetite Restored.

92 Church Street, Lowell, May 16, 1877.

Messrs. C. I. HOOD & Co.

Gents—Three months since I found myself very much reduced, had no appetite, no strength and was feeling as mean as any one could and be about my work. As soon as I began taking HOOD'S SARSAPARILLA my food relished and seemed to do me some good, which it did not before. I felt myself growing stronger every day, and am now feeling better than I have for a long time. I thoroughly believe in the value of Hood's Sarsaparilla.

Yours, etc. WM. H. MUNGAN.

PREPARED ONLY BY

C. I. HOOD & CO., Apothecaries,

Barristers' Hall, Lowell, Mass.

Sold by all druggists.

RAISED CAKE.

Three cups of light dough, three eggs, two heaping cups of sugar, one cup of butter, one cup of chopped raisins; put in a dish together and work with hand till well mixed, spice to taste. Put in pans and bake immediately.

Hood's Sarsaparilla gives an appetite.

CHEAP SPONGE CAKE.

Three eggs, one cup of sugar, one cup of flour, into which mix one teaspoonful of cream tartar, and one-half teaspoonful of soda dissolved in three teaspoonfuls of warm water. The last thing add a dessert spoonful of vinegar, stirring briskly. Bake about twenty-five minutes in not too hot an oven. The batter will be very thin.

MRS. S.'S SPONGE CAKE.

Eleven eggs, four cups of sugar, four cups of flour; beat the yolks and sugar together, add the whites well beaten, stir the flour in last as lightly as possible.

CORN STARCH CAKE.

The whites of three eggs, one-half cup of corn starch, one-half cup of butter, one-half cup of milk, one-half teaspoonful of cream tartar, one-fourth teaspoonful of soda, one cup of sugar, one cup of flour. Flavor with lemon.

Hood's Tooth Powder should be used by every one. .

ELECTION CAKE.

One pound of sugar, three-fourths of a pound of butter, four eggs, one-half pint of yeast, two and a half pounds of flour, one pint of milk, spices and raisins, one teacup of molasses; mix the yeast with the milk and part of the flour and let it stand over night; in the morning work the butter and sugar together, then add the eggs and work the dough with the rest of the ingredients; rise again before baking.

DELICIOUS CAKE.

Two cups of white sugar, one cup of butter, one cup of milk, three eggs, half teaspoonful of soda, one teaspoonful of cream tartar, three cups of flour; beat butter and sugar together, add the yolks of the eggs, then the beaten whites; dissolve the soda in milk, rub the cream tartar in flour and add last.

Hood's Sarsaparilla imparts new life to all the functions of the body.

CIRCLE CAKE.

One egg, one cup of sugar, two cups of flour, one-third of a cup of butter, one-half cup of sweet milk, one teaspoonful of cream tartar, one-half teaspoonful of soda. Flavor with rose or lemon.

PANCAKES.

One pint of milk, three eggs, one teaspoonful of salt; mix to a very thin batter, drop in hot lard. To be eaten with wine and sugar.

CHAPIN CAKE.

Six cups flour, one cup of butter, three cups of sugar, two cups of milk, two eggs, one teaspoonful of soda, one pound of chopped raisins.

Hood's Tooth Powder prevents the accumulation of tartar.

BUTTERMILK CAKE.

Three cups of pulverized sugar, one cup of butter, one cup of buttermilk, six eggs, one teaspoonful of soda, three cups of flour.

COFFEE CAKE.

Five cups of flour, one cup of butter, one cup of coffee, one cup of molasses, one cup of sugar, one cup of raisins, and a teaspoonful of soda.

Hood's Sarsaparilla cures dyspepsia.

TUSSANO.

TUS-SA-NO,

From the Latin words *Tussis*, COUGH — *Sano*, CURE.

COUGH CURE.

The cures effected by the use of Tussano prove conclusively that it contains valuable medicinal agents for the relief and permanent cure of Coughs, Colds, Hoarseness, Bronchitis, Sore Throat, Ministers' Sore Throat, Asthma, and all affections of the Throat and Lungs, including that dread destroyer of human life, Consumption, when it has not advanced beyond the reach of medicine. It loosens a cough and causes free and easy expectoration, removes inflammation, and by its wonderful soothing properties heals and strengthens the lungs. Tussano is composed of medicinal agents long and favorably known by all and held in the highest esteem by the most eminent men in the medical faculty in the treatment of these diseases. In exhausting the active properties from Wild Cherry, Thoroughwort and other ingredients of which Tussano is made, we employ the best methods known to Pharmacy and offer as a result a preparation of unsurpassed beauty, flavor and excellence, which make it the most desirable Cough Medicine ever offered to the people and adapt it particularly to the requirements of every family, especially where there are children. Official reports show the alarming facts that nearly one-fourth of the whole number of deaths are caused by Consumption and Pneumonia. These diseases are always preceded by a cough, which Tussano invariably cures, if it is used in season. Remember that "A stitch in time saves nine."

We challenge the world to produce a remedy equal to Tussano for the purposes for which it is designed. By long and careful study we have succeeded in compounding a purely vegetable preparation, combining rare curative properties in such proportion as to secure the positive effect of each. It is safe to use in all cases, and has proved itself an efficient remedy for all diseases of the Throat and Lungs from a slight Cold or Cough to Consumption in its incipient or advanced stage, affording great relief and permanently curing when it is possible for medicine to do so.

PREPARED BY

C. I. HOOD & CO., Apothecaries, Lowell, Mass.

Hood's Tooth Powder recommended by Dentists.

JELLY CAKE.

Three eggs, one cup of sugar, one cup of flour, small teaspoonful of cream tartar, half a teaspoonful of soda dissolved in two tablespoonfuls of milk; beat all well together. When baked spread with jelly.

Hood's Sarsaparilla cures dyspepsia.

TUMBLER CAKE.

Three tumblers of sugar, one tumbler of butter, one tumbler of sweet milk, four eggs, five tumblers of flour, one teaspoonful cream tartar, one-half teaspoonful soda, a tumbler of citron. Flavor with lemon.

PARK STREET CAKE.

Whites and yolks of four eggs beaten separately, two cups of white sugar, one cup of milk, three cups of flour, one-half cup butter, two teaspoonfuls of cream tartar, one teaspoonful of soda. Flavor to taste.

HICKORY NUT CAKE.

One cup of sugar, one-half cup butter, one-half cup milk, two cups flour, one teaspoonful cream tartar, one-half teaspoonful soda, one large cup raisins, one cup nuts broken up, two eggs.

Worthy of notice: Hood's Tooth Powder.

DELICATE CAKE.

Nearly three cups flour, two cups of sugar, three-fourths of a cup of sweet milk, whites of six eggs, one teaspoonful of cream tartar, half a teaspoonful of soda, half a cup of butter. Lemon for flavoring.

SKELETONS.

Two eggs, three tablespoonfuls of sugar and one tablespoonful of butter, flour to make very stiff. Roll very thin and cut in fancy shapes.

Hood's Sarsaparilla tones and strengthens the digestive organs.

RAISIN CAKE.

One-half cup of butter, one-half cup of sugar, two eggs, one-half cup of sweet milk, three cups of flour, one cup of raisins, one-half teaspoonful of soda, one teaspoonful of cream tartar.

Hood's Tooth Powder neutralizes the offensive secretions of the mouth.

MOLASSES GINGERBREAD, No. 1.

Two cups of Orleans molasses, one cup of sugar, one cup of sour milk, one-half cup of butter, one egg, one teaspoonful of soda, tablespoonful of ginger, sufficient flour for a thick batter.

MOLASSES GINGERBREAD, No. 2.

Two cups of molasses, one-half cup of butter, one cup of sour cream, one teaspoonful of ginger, two teaspoonfuls of soda, five and a half cups of flour.

HARD GINGERBREAD.

One cup of butter, two cups of sugar, three eggs, one teaspoonful of cream tartar, one-half teaspoonful soda. Season with ginger and nutmeg. Flour enough to roll.

GINGER SNAPS.

Bring to a scald one cup of molasses, and stir in one tablespoonful of soda, pour it, while foaming, over one cup of sugar, one egg, one tablespoonful of ginger, beaten together; then add one tablespoonful of vinegar. Flour enough to roll stirred in as lightly as possible.

Hood's Sarsaparilla works wonders in the blood.

DOUGHNUTS.

One quart flour, one egg, one-half cup sugar, one cup sweet milk, six teaspoonfuls melted lard, two even spoonfuls cream tartar, one even spoonful soda.

RAISED DOUGHNUTS.

Two cups of milk, half cup of yeast, flour enough to make a batter; make this batter at noon, set it in a warm place and let it rise until night; if light add tablespoonful of butter, same of salt, one egg, cup of sugar and a little cinnamon, half teaspoonful of soda, and let it rise until morning.

DOUGHNUTS, No. 2.

One cup of sour milk, one cup of sugar, one egg, one teaspoonful of soda, two tablespoonfuls melted butter, a little salt and spice. Mix very soft.

Hood's Tooth Powder should be used every night and morning.

COOKIES, No. 1.

Two cups of sugar, one cup of butter, two eggs, one half cup of milk, one teaspoonful of cream tartar, one-half teaspoonful of soda, flour to roll stiff.

COOKIES, No. 2.

One and a half cups of brown sugar, one cup of butter two eggs, one cup of currants, two great spoonfuls o sweet milk, small teaspoonful of soda; cinnamon, cloves nutmeg to taste.

BUNS.

Three cups new milk, one cup of sugar, one-half cup o yeast; make a stiff batter at night; in the morning mix one-half cup of butter and one and a half cups of sugar and mix with the batter, flour to roll out, add currants Cut out as biscuit, and raise them light before baking.

To build up the system use Hood's Sarsaparilla.

CURRANT WINE PIE.

One cup currant wine, one cup sugar, one spoonful o flour. Two crusts.

Read page 38,

CORROBORATED FACTS.

The Worst Case of Scrofulous Humor on Record Cured.

MESSRS. C. I. HOOD & Co. Lowell, Mass., Sept. 25, 1877.

My Dear Sirs :—If any one doubts what has been done for me by Hood's Sarsaparilla, I would like to have them call and see me. I take no stock in testimonials away off, but what has been done here is worth looking at. For nearly ten years past I have had scrofulous sores, from which I have suffered more than I can possibly tell. For nearly two years (previous to my taking Hood's Sarsaparilla) I have not been out of the house, as they came out on my limbs, and during the six months previous to May I was obliged to use crutches to get round my room. These sores seemed to be real ulcers, and were so called by doctors who examined them. One of them was so deep that it caused the muscles of my leg to contract so that I could not touch my heel to the floor. I had thirteen of these sores on me at one time. My health was very poor, appetite fastidious, thin in flesh and could not sleep nights on account of pain and nervousness. Mr. Moses Whittier urged me to try Hood's Sarsaparilla, and was so sanguine of its merit that I finally, with more faith in him than in the medicine, sent for a bottle. Am now taking the fourth bottle. Before I had taken the first bottle there was a great change in me, which was spoken of by others in the house. Before I had taken the third, the sores, six in number, and one very large one which the children said was a terrible sight, were nearly healed. My appetite has been better ever after I commenced taking the Sarsaparilla, am stronger, am regaining my flesh, sleep well and am in better health than I have been for years. Don't use crutches, can put my foot square upon the floor, and have been upon the street several times. Others are now taking the Sarsaparilla on my recommendation, and all are being benefited by it. Am willing you should publish these facts, for if others are suffering as I have, I would like them to know how much I have been relieved, for all of which I am sincerely grateful.

SARAH C. WHITTIER, No. 6 Tremont Corporation.

MESSRS. C. I. HOOD & Co. Lowell, Mass., Oct. 9, 1877.

Gentlemen :—In reply to your inquiry as to Miss Sarah Whittier, I would say, I have known her for more than twelve years. During the few years just passed she has been a constant sufferer from scrofulous sores, and was obliged to leave her work about three years ago on account of these sores. Late last spring I did not think it possible for her to live many months, at the longest. She was a mere skeleton, had scrofulous sores on her ear and limbs, and could put but one heel to the floor on account of a terrible sore on her leg, which had drawn up the muscles and cords. She could not get about her room except with the aid of crutches. I advised her to use Hood's Sarsaparilla. I saw her a few days since and found her very much improved; has regained her flesh, walks out on the street, without crutches; her changed condition is very remarkable. She has used four bottles Hood's Sarsaparilla. I give you this confirmation of her statement of the wonderful effect of Hood's Sarsaparilla upon her, h at others suffering may have reason to believe in the efficacy of this very excellent medicine. Respectfully yours,

MOSES WHITTIER, No. 23 Kirk Street.

WAFERS.

One quart of flour, four ounces of lard or butter, a littl salt. Mix with cold water; pound with a rolling pi twenty minutes. To be rolled out very thin, and cut wit a doughnut cutter. To be eaten with jelly.

Hood's Tooth Powder gives the gums a bright, health color.

FRUIT CAKE.

Two eggs, one and a half cups of molasses, one cup butter, one teaspoonful of cloves, one teaspoonful of ci namon, one-half teaspoonful of saleratus, three cups flour, one pound currants or raisins—improved by citro Bake two hours rather slowly.

CHEAP FRUIT CAKE.

One-half cup of butter, two cups of flour, three-fourtl of a cup of sugar, one-half cup of milk, less than one-ha cup of molasses, two eggs, one-half teaspoonful of sod in molasses to foam, one cup of chopped raisins, a littl clove and cinnamon.

LEMON CAKE.

One cup of butter, three cups of sugar rubbed to cream; stir into it the yolks of five well-beaten eggs, di: solve a teaspoonful of soda in a teacup of milk, then ad the milk and the grated peel of one lemon, the whites five eggs, sifting in as lightly as possible four teacupfu of flour. This will make four long tins full.

To invigorate the aged use Hood's Sarsaparilla.

CLOVE CAKE.

Two cups of flour, one-half cup of molasses, one-ha cup of butter, one-half cup of milk, two eggs, two cuj or more of raisins, one teaspoonful of soda, one-half tea spoonful each of cloves, cinnamon and alspice, one-half nutmeg.

A REAL BLOOD PURIFIER.

The *Lowell Weekly Journal* of May 11, says: "We do not as a rule allow ourselves to use our editorial columns to speak of any remedy we advertise, but we feel warranted in saying a word for HOOD'S SARSAPARILLA. Sarsaparilla has been known to materia medica as a remedial agent for centuries, and is recommended by all schools of practice as a valuable blood-purifier. It is put up in forms of almos' infinite variety; but Messrs. Hood & Co. who are thoroughly reliable pharmacists, seem to have hit upon a preparation of unusual value. Certainly they have vouchers for cures which *we know* to be most extraordinary."

Lost Twenty-Five Pounds.

A gentleman tells us: "Before I commenced taking HOOD'S SARSAPARILLA I had fallen in weight from 165 to 140 pounds. With the first bottle my appetite has returned, my strength is restored and I am rapidly regaining my flesh."

Gained Ten Pounds.

Another gentleman who has been suffering from the *debility* and *languor* peculiar to this season, says: "HOOD'S SARSAPARILLA is putting new life right into me. I have gained ten pounds since I began to take it." Has taken two bottles.

No other Sarsaparilla has such a sharpening effect upon the appetite. No other preparation tones and strengthens the digestive organs like HOOD'S SARSAPARILLA.

HOOD'S SARSAPARILLA works through the blood, *regulating, toning* and *invigorating* all the functions of the body.

Wonderful cases of Scrofulous Humor cured prove more than we ever claimed for HOOD'S SARSAPARILLA.

An ex-alderman of this city says of HOOD'S SARSAPARILLA, "It is the strongest Sarsaparilla I ever saw."

Persistent cases of Scrofula have yielded to HOOD'S SARSAPARILLA.

Sold by all druggists.

PREPARED ONLY BY

C. I. HOOD & CO., Apothecaries,

Barristers' Hall, Lowell, Mass.

WEDDING CAKE.

Two pounds each of butter, sugar and flour, six pounds of currants, five of raisins, and two of citron, and nineteen eggs, two tablespoonfuls of cloves, six nutmegs. wineglass of brandy.

ICE CREAM CAKE.

Whites of five eggs, one and a half cups of sugar, one-half cup of butter, one cup of milk, one-half teaspoonful of soda, one teaspoonful of cream tartar, three cups flour. Separate this mixture and color half with strawberry coloring. Flavor this with vanilla, the white with lemon. Put in the white, then the pink. Bake slowly.

Invest 25 cents in a bottle of Hood's Tooth Powder.

NEW YORK CUP CAKE.

Take four eggs, four tumblers of sifted flour, three tumblers of powdered white sugar, one tumbler of butter, one tumbler of rich milk, one glass of white wine, a grated nutmeg, a teaspoonful of powdered cinnamon, and a small teaspoonful of saleratus. Warm the milk and cut in the butter, keeping it by the fire until the butter is melted: stir into the milk the eggs beaten very light, in turn with the flour; add the spice and wine, and lastly, the saleratus dissolved in a little vinegar. Stir it all very hard. Bake in a loaf, in a moderate oven.

This is a good time to take Hood's Sarsaparilla.

QUEEN OF PUDDINGS.

One pint of nice bread crumbs, one quart of milk, one cup of sugar, the yolks of four eggs, the grated rind of one lemon, a piece of butter the size of an egg. Baked like a custard. When baked spread over the top slices of jelly of any kind, and cover the whole with the whites of the eggs beaten to a stiff froth, with one cup of sugar and the juice of the lemon. Brown lightly in the oven.

FOUR FRUIT PUDDING.

Butter thin slices of baker's bread on both sides. Stew together raspberries, blueberries, blackberries and currants, and sweeten to taste. Fill the pudding dish with a layer of bread and a layer of fruit, alternately, and cover the top with a frosting of whites of eggs beaten with sugar. Set it in the oven long enough to brown the frosting delicately. This is best prepared the day before it is to be eaten. It is to be served with cream if convenient.

To remove all humors of the blood use Hood's Sarsaparilla.

ORANGE PUDDING.

Six oranges pared and cut fine, strew over them one cup of sugar, beat the yolks of six eggs with four spoonfuls of corn starch, strain into one quart of boiling milk, put the starch over the oranges when hot. Beat the whites of the eggs with two spoonfuls of sugar, and pour them over the starch. Brown in the oven. To be eaten cold.

Decorate your mouth with pearly teeth by using Hood's Tooth Powder.

LEMON PUDDING.

The yolks of three eggs, beaten with nine spoonfuls of white sugar, the juice of two lemons, a tablespoonful of flour, two spoonfuls of melted butter, a small tumbler of sweet milk. Make a batter for a pie, after it is baked and ready, beat to a froth the whites of three eggs, with three spoonfuls of white sugar, spread it over the top and return to the oven and brown lightly.

DELMONT PUDDING.

Set one quart of milk into water and let it boil, beat the yolks of five eggs with four tablespoonfuls of corn starch, one cup of sugar. Cook in the milk and flavor to taste. Beat the whites of the five eggs with one-half cup of sugar, flavor and pour over the top. Set in the oven till lightly browned.

Hood's Sarsaparilla restores and renovates the whole system.

SUET PUDDING.

One cup of chopped raisins, two cups of suet, one cup of sweet milk, two-thirds of a cup of molasses, one teaspoonful of soda, four cups of flour. Steam two hours. Wine sauce.

COTTAGE PUDDING WITH SAUCE.

One coffee cup of sugar, one tablespoonful butter, two eggs, three cups flour, one cup milk, two even spoonfuls of cream tartar, one even spoonful soda.

Trial bottle Hood's Sarsaparilla 50 cts. Large bottles $1.00.

PEACH PIE.

Select mellow, juicy peaches; wash and place them in a deep pie plate lined with paste; strew a thick layer of sugar over each of the peaches, adding a spoonful of water and sprinkling of flour over the top of each layer; cover with a thick crust, and bake about an hour.

CREAM PIES.

One quart of milk, the yolks of three eggs, two cups of sugar, two spoonfuls of flour; boil this until it begins to thicken. Make a rich crust, put in the cream, flavor with lemon, and bake in a quick oven. Beat the whites of the eggs stiff, and frost. Put in the oven and color a little.

Make your children clean their teeth with Hood's Tooth Powder.

CREAM OR COCOANUT PIES.

Two eggs, one cup of sugar, one-half cup of water, one-half teaspoonful of soda dissolved in the water, one teaspoonful cream tartar, one and a half cups of flour, a small lump of butter. Cream—one-half cup of sugar, one-half cup of flour, one egg; beat the egg, stir in the sugar and flour, then stir in one-half pint boiling milk, and two spoonfuls cocoanut. Make a frosting for the outside, sprinkle thickly with cocoanut before dry. The pie will be delicious.

Read page 23 ; it may save a friend's life.

A dentist who has had a large practice in our city for many years, writes us regarding

Hood's Tooth Powder.

LOWELL, MASS., Sept. 25th, 1877.

MESSRS. C. I. HOOD & CO.

Gentlemen:—Since you began to manufacture Hood's Saponaceous Tooth Powder I have used it in my family and have recommended it in my practice extensively. I regard it as one of the best dentifrices in the market, and knowing the materials and the careful manner in which it is made, I can assure the public that it contains nothing that can possibly injure the teeth or gums, but if used constantly will cleanse and preserve them, and its neutralizing properties will keep the mouth sweet.

Yours truly,

A. T. JOHNSON, DENTIST.

———

Wonderful Stories are told over our counter of what Hood's Sarsaparilla has done and is doing.

A lady full of animation said to us, "I have not been able to work constantly during the hot weather for many years. This summer I have taken three bottles Hood's Sarsaparilla, and have been vigorous and strong through the hot weather, and have worked every day, and feel as smart and active now as can be."

This is only one of many.

Hood's Sarsaparilla eradicates scrofula.

ROXBURY PATENT CREAM PIE.

One and one-half cups sugar, one and one-half cups flour, five eggs and a little lemon. Beat the yolks and sugar well, then add the whites previously beaten to a stiff froth with the flour. Fill with the following : to a pint of boiling milk add one-half cup sugar and one-half cup of flour. Beat with two eggs and a little lemon. Let it boil two or three minutes, and set in a cool place.

LEMON PIE, No. 1.

Two lemons, two cups sugar, five eggs, two tablespoonfuls of corn starch, one pint of milk ; grate the lemons, add the juice, stir together. Scald the corn starch with milk. This will make two pies, which must be baked in rich puff paste.

Hood's Sarsaparilla is the best, strongest and cheapest.

LEMON PIE, No. 2.

Grate the rind of one lemon for spice, press out the juice and add to it one cup of powdered sugar, the yolks of two eggs, and one whole egg, one teaspoonful of corn starch scalded in one-half cup of milk. Line a deep plate with pastry, and pour in the mixture ; bake like a custard pie. While this is baking beat the whites of two eggs with three tablespoonfuls of sugar to a stiff froth. When the pie is done pour on the frosting, return to the oven and brown lightly.

RAISIN PIE.

Boil one pound raisins an hour covered with water, add one lemon, one cup white sugar, two tablespoonfuls of flour. For three pies.

A Georgia girl says Hood's Tooth Powder is the best.

SAUCE.

Two cups sugar, one cup butter, wine glass wine, two eggs. Pour over boiling water ; to be well beaten.

Hood's Sarsaparilla has cured salt rheum.

APPLE PUFFS.

Pare and slice six tart apples, stew them and strain them through a cullender, sweeten and add a pinch of salt; let this cool while you make your paste, of two spoonfuls of butter worked into eight spoonfuls of flour; add ice water to make consistency of bread dough, put on the molding board and roll quite thin, scatter small pieces of butter over this, and dredge with flour, then fold it up and roll quite thin again, repeat this operation any number of times, always rolling the paste into something like a square form. Cut the paste into pieces four inches square, put a small spoonful of sauce on one-half of the square, moisten the paste around it with water, and fold the other half over on to it. Make the edges perfectly smooth. Bake in a dripping pan lined with paper in a quick oven. When you take them from the oven sift a little powdered sugar over each puff.

It is delightful to cleanse the teeth with Hood's Tooth Powder.

GOLD AND SILVER PUDDING.

One quart of milk, one cup of sugar, six eggs, leaving out the whites of four; scald the milk; add sugar and dissolved corn starch, and one wineglass of Sherry wine; bake for half an hour; when cold cover with a frosting made of the whites of the four eggs, a cup of pulverized sugar, and flavoring; brown in a hot oven.

Scrofula and salt rheum have been cured by Hood's Sarsaparilla.

RICE PUDDING.

One cup of rice boiled soft in water; add a pint of cold milk and a piece of butter size of an egg, yolks of four eggs, rind of lemon grated. Mix and bake half an hour. Beat the whites of four eggs; stir in a pint of sugar, the juice of a lemon. After the pudding is baked and cooled a little, pour this over and brown in oven. Eat cold. Will keep several days.

32

The *Lowell Daily Courier* of June 3rd, 1876, says Hood's Sarsaparilla "is fast growing into use, and doing much good. This is no 'patent medicine,' but a preparation of a standard article for specific diseases, and its effect is said to be very marked. The testimonials which they give are bona fide from parties who have used the preparation, and cheerfully give their testimony as to its worth. Those afflicted with Scrofula, Liliousness or general debility should try this remedy. Hood & Co. are careful and experienced pharmacists, and their preparations can be relied on."

Dyspepsia and Sick Headache.

Lowell, Mass., June 10, 1878.

Messrs. C. I. HOOD & Co.

Gentlemen — For over a year I have suffered constantly from sick headache and dyspepsia; have tried remedies without benefit. Before I had taken two bottles of HOOD'S SARSAPARILLA I was much better. I am rarely troubled with headache now, and my food does not distress me as it did. It has done me good, and I cheerfully recommend it. Very truly yours,
HELEN J. MORRILL, No. 133 Cross Street.

SCIATICA RHEUMATISM.

Lowell, June, 1878.

Messrs. C. I. HOOD & Co.

Gentlemen — Two years ago this fall I had an attack of Sciatica Rheumatism, which confined me to the house three months, but really kept about me a whole year, when I was taken down again. This time it hung on for five weeks. Then I commenced taking HOOD'S SARSAPARILLA. The first two bottles didn't seem to do me any good, excepting my appetite; but when I commenced on the third I found it was fixing me all right. The pain left my leg entirely, but a strip two inches wide from my hip to my heel continued numb. This has all gone excepting on the heel and side of my foot, which is so slight I hardly notice it. I had no appetite till I took your Sarsaparilla. In the morning I had a faint feeling at my stomach, and before noon I would be nearly exhausted. HOOD'S SARSAPARILLA has entirely overcome all these troubles and given me such an appetite that I can eat anything. My folks are fearful I shall have it again this fall, but I tell them I shall bridge it over with HOOD'S SARSAPARILLA. I know where 18 bottles of your Sarsaparilla have been used, and every one given perfect satisfaction.

With my best wishes for the success of your valuable medicine, I am very truly yours. AARON JACOBS, 31 Congress Street.

Hood's Sarsaparilla is sold by all Druggists.
$1.00 a bottle, or six large bottles for $5.00. Trial size, 50 cents.

C. I. HOOD & CO., Apothecaries, Lowell, Mass.

Hood's Tooth Powder preserves the teeth.

GERMAN TOAST.

Cut into slices a loaf of baker's bread, soak them ten or fifteen minutes in a pint of milk, two eggs and a little salt. Fry in equal parts of lard and butter till they are a light brown on both sides. This dish is quickly prepared for a dessert and may be eaten with a pudding sauce.

COTTAGE PUDDING.

One cup of sugar, one cup of milk, butter the size of an egg, three eggs—reserving the whites of two for frosting— one pint of flour, one teaspoonful of cream tartar, one-half teaspoonful soda. When baked frost at once, with a cup of sugar added to the whites of the two eggs.

For your children use Hood's Sarsaparilla.

PLUM PUDDING.

Beat four eggs; stir to them half a pound of flour, and half a pint of milk, half a pound of chopped suet, half a pound of stoned raisins, well floured, and a few currants, a teaspoonful of salt. Boil the pudding four hours, briskly. Serve with wine sauce.

ENGLISH PUDDING.

One cup of molasses, one-half cup of butter, one cup of sweet milk, a teaspoonful of soda, a teaspoonful of different spices, one cup of chopped raisins, three and a half cups of flour. Steam two or three hours.

Thousands use Hood's Tooth Powder, and praise it.

VICTORIA FRITTERS.

Slice a loaf of baker's bread into pieces an inch thick; cut the slices in the center, trimming off the crust, and place them on a flat dish. Take a quart of rich milk, one salt-spoonful of salt, eight beaten eggs. Stir the whole together and pour over the bread several hours before dinner, that it may be equally moistened. Fry in hot butter a delicate brown, and eat with sweet wine sauce.

Hood's Sarsaparilla gives tone to the stomach.

HOOD'S
VEGETABLE PILLS.

25 CTS. A BOX; 5 BOXES FOR $1.00.

Sent by Mail to any Address on Receipt of Price.

PREPARED ONLY BY

C. I. HOOD & CO., Apothecaries,
LOWELL, MASS.

————◆◇◆————

HOOD'S VEGETABLE PILLS are made to meet a legitimate demand for a family physic that is perfectly safe and can be relied upon to do its work thoroughly. It is customary, and a wise custom it is, and, in fact, actually necessary, for every one to have on hand a physic of some kind, ready for immediate use. The necessity which so often compels all to resort to a medicine of this kind, renders it the most important one in the medicine-closet.

A fever is often warded off by the timely use of an efficient cathartic like HOOD'S VEGETABLE PILLS.

A cold is often annihilated in a single night by a dose of HOOD'S VEGETABLE PILLS, which might otherwise continue for days.

HOOD'S VEGETABLE PILLS are a mild, efficient cathartic, acting with certainty upon the liver, removing all obstructions from the alimentary canal and preventing all diseases arising from derangements of the liver and bowels.

CAUTION.—Avoid all pills containing calomel, mercury or any mineral substance, as they are liable to do harm.

Hood's Pills are a purely vegetable combination, and contain no calomel, mercury or mineral substance of any kind. We believe they are the best family physic that can be made, and offer them with perfect confidence, believing that whenever used it will be with the happiest results. Try them, and judge for yourself. Sent by mail to any address.

C. I. HOOD & CO., Apothecaries, Lowell, Mass.

————————————————

Hood's Sarsaparilla eradicates scrofula.

COCOANUT PIE.

One-half cup of butter, one and a half cups of white sugar, yolks of four eggs, and one whole egg, one-half cup of sweet milk, one-half teaspoonful of soda, one teaspoonful of cream tartar, two cups of flour; bake in thin pie pans. After beating the white to a stiff froth, stir in a cupful of sugar and a cupful of dessicated cocoanut, Put this between the layers of cake. Frosting improves it,

SALEM PUDDING.

One cup of suet chopped fine, one cup molasses, a little salt, one cup of milk, two teaspoonfuls cream tartar, one cup of raisins, one teaspoonful of soda, three and a half cups of flour. Steam three hours.

Hood's Tooth Powder is praised by everybody,

PUDDING SAUCE, No. 1.

One cup of sugar, one-half cup of butter, beaten to a cream; then add the yolk and white of one egg, beaten separately; flavor with a little lemon or vanilla; set to cool.

PUDDING SAUCE, No. 2.

Two eggs, one cup of sugar, one-half cup of butter, one cup of boiling wine, to be poured on the mixture thoroughly.

PUDDING SAUCE, No. 3.

Take the yolks of two eggs and a cup of sugar; beat five minutes and set over a teakettle to dissolve. When sufficiently thin for sauce, place in the dish ready to serve; then add the whites beaten to a stiff froth, and a wineglass of sherry.

A reliable and remarkable medicine : Hood's Sarsaparilla.

EGG SAUCE.

One egg, one cup of sugar well beaten with the egg, one-half cup boiling water, just before serving. Season to taste.

CARAMELS, No. 1.

Equal quantities of milk, sugar, molasses and chocolate. Put a little butter into a kettle and boil it like candy.

CARAMELS, No. 2.

One-half cup of molasses, one cup of sugar, one-half cup of milk, one-half spoonful of flour, butter one-half size of an egg, one-fourth of a pound of chocolate. Boil until hard, turn it into a pan, mark into squares.

If you expect to save your teeth, use Hood's Tooth Powder.

ENGLISH GELATINE.

To one paper of gelatine containing an ounce and a half, put a pint of cold water, after fifteen minutes add one quart of boiling water and stir until the gelatine is dissolved; then add a coffee cup of sugar, juice of lemon, or any spice or essence preferred, and boil it a minute. If the jelly is for an invalid, omit the lemon and use two gills of wine after it is boiled.

ORANGE GELATINE.

One ounce Cox's gelatine dissolved in one pint of hot water. When cool, add the juice of six oranges and two lemons. Strain the whole through a fine sieve and let it partially harden, then beat up the whites of two eggs, add them to the mixture and beat the whole five minutes or more, till stiff. Then put in a mould.

Hood's Sarsaparilla is the best, strongest and cheapest.

WINE JELLY, No. 1.

To one paper Cox's gelatine add one pint of cold water, the juice and grated rind of two lemons, one pounded nutmeg and two or three sticks of cinnamon. Allow this to stand one hour, then add one quart of boiling water, one pint of wine—Sherry is much the best—one wineglass of brandy, two pounds of white sugar. When all is dissolved strain through a flannel jelly bag.

Children like Hood's Sarsaparilla.

WINE JELLY, No. 2.

One-third of a package of gelatine dissolved in a little cold water; to this add a pint of hot water and let it come to a boil; then put in two cups of sugar, one-half cup of wine or boiled cider, and nearly one tablespoonful of essence of lemon. Let cool till the next day.

COFFEE CUSTARD.

One pint of strong coffee, one pint of milk, boiled together; six eggs, beaten with a cup and a half of sugar.

An agreeable remedy to take : Hood's Sarsaparilla.

CHOCOLATE CUSTARD.

One quart of milk, two eggs, two and a half heaping tablespoonfuls of corn starch or maizena, two tablespoonfuls of grated chocolate, six tablespoonfuls of sugar. Heat the milk almost to boiling —same as for soft custard. Beat the eggs, then add the corn starch and work it in till free from lumps; then add the chocolate, then sugar, and wet the whole with cold milk—take sufficient milk besides the quart to have it thin enough to pour—then pour the whole into the hot milk and stir until about as thick as soft custard. Let it cool a little and pour into glasses.

CHOCOLATE CANDY.

One cup grated chocolate, one cup milk, one cup molasses, butter size of an egg, one cup of sugar. Boil an hour.

Have you ever tried Hood's Tooth Powder?

TAPIOCA CREAMS, No. 1.

Wash and soak over night two tablespoonfuls of tapioca in cold water, drain off the water in the morning; beat the yolks of three eggs, mix them and the tapioca with a quart of milk, put on the stove and stir it, boil about two minutes. Sweeten and flavor to taste. When nearly cold, add the whites of the eggs, beaten stiff, stir in lightly and well. Serve in glass custard cups.

Hood's Sarsaparilla, the best spring medicine.

ARE YOU AWARE

That in your blood the taint of scrofula has a prominent place? This is true of every one. It is liable at any time, on the slightest provocation, to develope itself in some insidious disease. Consumption and many other diseases are outgrowths of this impurity of the blood. **HOOD'S SARSAPARILLA** has a wonderful power over all scrofulous troubles, as the remarkable testimonials published unmistakably prove.

Scrofulous Bunch in the Neck Removed.

DRACUT CENTRE, Oct. 13th, 1877.

MESSRS. C. I. HOOD & CO.

Dear Sirs:—About the first of last June I began to be troubled with a scrofula bunch on my neck, which so rapidly increased in size that I became alarmed. Knowing of a bad case of scrofula that had been cured with Hood's Sarsaparilla, I determined to give it a trial. I commenced taking the Sarsaparilla, and at the end of a week I found the bunch very much reduced. I continued using the Sarsaparilla until the bottle was finished, and by that time the bunch had almost entirely disappeared—being about the size of a pea. I think one more bottle will entirely cure me. I take great pleasure in adding my testimonial to the many remarkable ones you are receiving.

Sincerely yours, MARIA S. KIMBALL.

"We are All Going to Take It."

LOWELL, July 24, 1877.

MESSRS. C. I. HOOD & CO.

Gentlemen:—Last May my attention was called to the remarkable cures of Hood's Sarsaparilla. My daughter at that time was suffering with the worst case of scrofulous humor I ever saw. For several months she had a sore on her side as large as a good-sized dinner plate, which discharged a watery matter, which would dry and form a crust during the night. She was obliged to protect it by linen pinned to her clothing. Some nights it would itch so intensely she could not sleep. I got a bottle of Hood's Sarsaparilla and a box of Hood's Olive Ointment, and gave her half a teaspoonful of the Sarsaparilla three times a day, after eating, and applied the Ointment at night. We followed this course faithfully; in ten days it began to improve, and in five weeks it was entirely healed. The Ointment relieved the itching instantly. The dose being so small, it did not prove an expensive remedy, as one bottle performed the above cure. She will continue to take it through the summer and fall. I want two bottles; one for my sister, the other for myself and daughter, for we are all going to take it. Yours, &c., MRS. J. H. CONANT, 144 Merrimack Corporation, Colburn Street.

Hood's Tooth Powder preserves the teeth.

TAPIOCA CREAMS, No. 2.

Cover three tablespoonfuls of tapioca over night with water; pour off the water, if any, and put into one quart of milk over the fire; when it boils stir in the yolks of three eggs, two-thirds cup of sugar, a little salt, stir till it begins to thicken. Make a frosting of the whites of the eggs and spread over the top, sprinkle a little sugar over it and brown in the oven.

A Georgia girl says Hood's Tooth Powder is the best.

CHARLOTTE RUSSE, No. 1.

One-half pint of thick cream whipped to a froth, the whites of two eggs beaten to a froth, one cup of water with two spoonfuls of gelatine dissolved in it; sweeten to taste and flavor with vanilla or lemon. One loaf sponge cake, take a deep dish, line the dish with small strips of this cake, and pour the cream into the middle of the dish, put writing paper on the bottom of the dish. Let it remain until hardened, turn it out on a flat dish.

This is a good time to take Hood's Sarsaparilla.

CHARLOTTE RUSSE, No. 2.

Add six eggs well beaten to one quart boiling milk, one coffee cup of sugar, a bit of salt; flavor to suit the taste with vanilla and a little brandy, then add one box of gelatine dissolved in a pint of water. Set it away to cool and when it becomes the consistency of thick custard, add a pint of cream well beaten to a light froth. The gelatine must be warm when added to the custard, otherwise the jelly will be in lumps. Line the mould with small pieces of sponge cake, fill and put in a cool place.

VELVET CREAM, No. 1.

One box of gelatine with a teacup of wine poured over it; set this over a teakettle of boiling water until dissolved; one quart of cream sweetened with a coffee cup of sugar, into this pour dissolved gelatine, strain and pour in moulds to harden.

Hood's Sarsaparilla restores and renovates the whole system.

40

VELVET CREAM, No. 2.

Put one-half box of gelatine in one quart of milk, with the yolks of three eggs, on the stove; stir until it comes to a soft custard. When cold beat the whites of the eggs to a froth, add six tablespoonfuls of white sugar, one of flavoring, and stir in the mixture.

Make your children clean their teeth with Hood's Tooth Powder.

LEMON JELLY.

One quart of water, four tablespoonfuls of corn starch, one coffee cup white sugar, flavor to taste with lemon. Dissolve the sugar in the lemon, also the starch; cook as you would for boiled custards; when cooked turn into an earthen dish; let cool and then slip it into a platter. Beat the white of one egg with two tablespoonfuls of sugar, spread this over the top of the jelly, put in the oven and brown slightly. Serve with cream and sugar.

CHOCOLATE CREAMS.

Take half a cake of unsweetened chocolate, grate and set over the teakettle; while hot, drop in the cream moulds, which are made of two cups of sugar and half a cup of water; boil three minutes; after it begins to bubble remove from the stove and flavor with vanilla, stir until cold enough to make into moulds; after the chocolate is added put them on buttered paper to harden.

Hood's Sarsaparilla cures scrofulous humors.

A DISH OF SNOW.

Select very juicy apples, pare and core them, stew them in clear water until soft; strain through a sieve, sweeten to tase with powdered sugar. Spread this when cold in a deep glass dish. To every apple allow the white of one egg; beat the whites—with a tablespoonful of powdered sugar to one egg—to a stiff froth, and pour it over the apples. Any flavoring may be used.

Thousands praise Hood's Sarsaparilla.

THE PROSTRATION WHICH FOLLOWS
Diphtheria and Scarlet Fever,

And the persistency with which they cling to the patient, are well known to all who have had any experience with these terrible diseases. The following letters show how the restoring and invigorating properties of HOOD'S SARSAPARILLA overcome them, and how by vitalizing and enriching the blood it neutralizes and eradicates the poisoned matter from it, bringing to the convalescent the color, life and vigor of robust health. (See page 46.)

A new use has been found for HOOD'S SARSAPARILLA, or rather its application as a blood-purifier has been made in a new sort of cases. It is well known that diphtheria is a disease of a poisonous nature, and it frequently leaves the system of its victims tainted with its virus. As will be seen by a testimonial elsewhere (see page 46), the Sarsaparilla has been found to work a radical cure in a system debilitated and poisoned by this disease. The statement is a reasonable one and deserves attention.—*Lowell Daily Courier.*

Scarlet Fever.

LOWELL, MASS., March 16, 1878.

MESSRS. C. I. HOOD & CO.:

Gentlemen—Allow me the pleasure of saying one word in favor of HOOD'S SARSAPARILLA for the benefit of those suffering. Two years ago my daughter Mabel had scarlet fever in its worst form, so bad that some of her finger-nails came off. Her physician gave her up, saying he had done all he could for her; but she finally pulled through. It left her in a very prostrated condition, with a running sore on her left ear, the discharge being very offensive, also a difficulty of breathing through her nose, which disturbed her sleeping, waking her frequently during the night and annoying her very life out of her. She continued in about this way up to the time we tried your Sarsaparilla. We used various medicines, but nothing seemed to hit her case. Seeing Mrs. Sanborn's testimonial, and being acquainted with the circumstances, we thought possibly HOOD'S SARSAPARILLA might do Mabel good. I bought a bottle, and she began to use it. Her appetite, which had been dainty, improved at once, and she ate with a decided relish; the offensive discharge stopped; the sore healed; the trouble in the nose has entirely disappeared so that she sleeps like a log and breathes without difficulty. It has produced a complete renovation in her health. We are exceedingly happy to see her growing positively better every day. The child's appreciation of the medicine is quite remarkable; as for our own, we leave it for you and others to judge.

Very truly yours,
ALBERT E. LIBBY,
32 Third, cor. Read St.

C. I. HOOD & CO., *Apothecaries, Lowell, Mass.*

Trial bottle, 50 cents; large bottle, $1.00; six bottles for $5.00.

The Best family physic—Hood's Vegetable Pills.

ICE CREAM, No. 1.

One quart of new milk, one quart of cream, four eggs, three-fourths of a pound of sugar. Boil the milk, and add eggs and sugar well beaten together. When cold add flavoring and freeze.

ICE CREAM, No. 2.

One quart of cream, one pint of milk, one cup of sugar; flavor to taste. Beat the cream to a froth; stir in the milk and sugar thoroughly and freeze.

Worthy of notice : Hood's Tooth Powder.

FROSTING.

Whites of two eggs beaten to a froth; add a cup of sugar and tablespoonful of powdered starch.

CHOCOLATE FROSTING.

Two squares of chocolate, one and a half cups of sugar, one-half cup of boiling water. Let it boil fifteen minutes.

SPANISH CREAM.

Dissolve one-third of a box of gelatine in three-fourths of a quart of milk for one hour, then put on the stove, and when boiling, stir in the yolks of three eggs beaten with three-fourths of a cup of sugar; when it is boiling hot remove from the fire, and stir in the whites of three eggs well beaten. Flavor to taste; pour in moulds.

Hood's Tooth Powder neutralizes the offensive secretions of the mouth.

FRICANDELLES.

Take cold beef, veal, or any other meat, the more variety the better, hash it fine, and mix with it two eggs, a little grated onion, melted butter, two crackers pounded, pepper, salt. Form into balls and fry in butter. Serve with drawn butter flavored with lemon.

Invest 25 cents in a bottle of Hood's Tooth Powder.

SPICED BEEF.

Five pounds of the shank, boiled five hours, with celery seed. Drain off the gelatine then, and chop the meat very fine, add pepper and salt to taste, and put it into a cloth, on a platter. Cover it with the cloth and press it.

Hood's Sarsaparilla works wonders in the blood.

SPICED BEEF, To Serve Hot.

Fry three or four slices of pork a light brown; then lay in the beef (the round is good for this purpose) in one piece. Let it brown a little on both sides; then cover it with water, and let it stew over a moderate fire four or five hours in a covered kettle. Add water when it boils away to make gravy. About half an hour before it is done, salt and pepper it to taste; add one teaspoonful of sweet marjoram, and if agreeable, one-half of an onion sliced. Pour the gravy over the beef when serving it.

BAKED OMELET.

Heat three gills of milk with a dessert spoonful of butter in it; beat thoroughly four or five eggs; wet a tablespoonful of flour and a teaspoonful of salt in a little cold milk. Mix the eggs with the flour and cold milk, then add the hot milk, stirring fast. Bake in a quick oven fifteen or twenty minutes.

Hood's Tooth Powder prevents the accumulation of tartar.

VEAL LOAF.

Take three and one-half pounds of veal, fat and lean, one thick slice of fat salt pork; chop the whole raw; take six common crackers pounded fine, two eggs, one-half cup of butter, one tablespoonful of pepper, a little clove, and any herb to suit the taste. Mix all well together, and make into a loaf like bread; put into a shallow baking pan with a little water, cover with bits of butter, and dredge flour over it; bake slowly two hours, basting it as you would meat. This is nice cut in thin slices for a tea dish, and it will keep good for some time.

Indigestion and Debility Permanently Cured.

MESSRS. C. I. HOOD & CO.

Gentlemen:—Seriously opposed to all patent medicines, it was after a great deal of talk that I was persuaded to try Hood's Sarsaparilla for my wife, who has been troubled with indigestion and debility for several years, which had really rendered her feeble. Finally I was induced, faithlessly, to try one bottle of Hood's Sarsaparilla. Before she had taken all of this her health commenced to improve. She is now taking the fourth bottle, and her health has steadily and permanently improved, and I firmly believe Hood's Sarsaparilla is entitled to the credit, and I most cheerfully and confidently recommend it to any and all suffering.

GEO. W. BOSWORTH.

Amherst, N. H., Sept. 18, 1877.

☞ HOOD'S SARSAPARILLA is a combination of remedies whose special adaptation to the cure of scrofula and cleansing the blood of impurities has been thoroughly proven by time and trial.

HUMOR IN THE NOSE CURED.

"Pleasant to Take."

LOWELL, Mass., Oct. 1, 1877.

MESSRS. C. I. HOOD & CO.

Dear Sirs:—Last fall my boy had a humor develop itself around his finger nails which would fester up, become very sore and the nail come off; finally it left his fingers and went to his nose, first inside, and at last reaching down on the outside of the nostril, near the lip. We used various remedies without benefit. His general health became very much impaired. I went to my family physician (Dr. Green), and he ordered sarsaparilla. I got a bottle of your make (Hood's Sarsaparilla) and in five or six weeks it began to heal and continued to steadily till entirely well, and his sickly, puny look changed to one of vigor and health. He has taken it most of the time since, as I am desirous of eradicating this humor entirely from his blood. It is exceedingly commendatory of your Sarsaparilla that it is so pleasant to take that he really likes it and will call for it.

Very truly yours,

JOHN G. ROGERS.

(Firm of Stiles, Rogers & Co., Flour, Grain, &c., Market Street.)

Hood's Tooth Powder is perfectly safe.

OMELET.

Six eggs; beat the yolks and whites separately, one table-spoonful flour, mix smoothly with a little milk, a little salt, one small teacup sweet milk. Beat all thoroughly together, adding the whites last. Pour into a buttered spider; when partly done, double it like a turnover.

OMELET SOUFFLE.

One pint sweet milk, made boiling hot, one cup of flour, mixed very smoothly in a little cold milk, one spoonful sugar, piece of butter size of a walnut. Stir all into the boiling milk till it is quite stiff (this can be done early in the morning.) When cool stir in the yolks of five eggs, thoroughly beaten, adding the whites last, also thoroughly beaten. Bake half an hour.

Hood's Sarsaparilla gives an appetite.

HODGE PODGE.

Four quarts chopped green tomatoes, one quart chopped onions, one coffee cup chopped green peppers, one coffee cup white mustard seed, one coffee cup salt. Put the salt on the tomatoes and let stand over night; drain them and add the other ingredients. Cover the whole with cold, sharp vinegar.

FOR CURING TONGUE OR BEEF.

One-half ounce of potash, one-half ounce saltpetre, one pound brown sugar, one and a half pounds of rock salt. For twenty-five or thirty pounds.

Hood's Tooth Powder should be used by every one.

PICKLE FOR HAM.

Four gallons water, six pounds salt, two and a half pounds of sugar, two and a half ounces saltpetre. Boil and skim the pickles; put the hams in when perfectly cold; let them remain in the pickle six weeks. This is sufficient for fifty or sixty pounds.

Hood's Sarsaparilla works wonders in the blood.

DIPHTHERIA.

MESSRS. C. I. HOOD & CO., Lowell, Mass.:

Gentlemen—My little girl had the diphtheria last April. The disease left her very weak, blood poor, with no appetite, and she could not seem to rally from its effects. HOOD'S SARSAPARILLA was recommended by a neighbor. After she had been taking it a few days we noticed a change for the better—she began to eat with a relish. It seemed to take out the poison the disease had left in her blood, the change being very noticeable in her face. She took it two months and fully regained her health, much to our delight. We now recommend HOOD'S SARSAPARILLA with a great deal of pleasure.

Very truly yours,
J. R. SMITH,
19 Butterfield St., Lowell, Mass.

KIDNEY COMPLAINT.

DRACUT, MASS., March 18, 1878.

MESSRS. C. I. HOOD & CO., Lowell, Mass.:

Dear Sirs—I have suffered from kidney complaint and biliousness for fifteen years. Have tried everything and never got any good. Last January, before I commenced taking HOOD'S SARSAPARILLA, everything I ate bloated me all up; pain in my chest and arms, backache, dizzy. I could not get up without feeling weary and all lagged out. Many mornings I was obliged to lie down on the lounge. To do any work seemed almost impossible. Have taken two bottles. That backache, dizziness, pain in the chest and arms, and that feeling of intense weariness, are all gone. I can eat anything, and it does not press me at all. Feel just like work—in fact, like a new man. Can heartily recommend HOOD'S SARSAPARILLA, and hope all who desire to know anything about it, will come to me and ask what I think of it.

Very truly yours,
JONATHAN J. COBURN.

Hood's Sarsaparilla is 50 Cts. Trial Size; $1 Regular Size; Six Bottles for $5.

C. I. HOOD & CO., Apothecaries,

LOWELL, MASS.

Try Hood's Vegetable Pills, a purely vegetable cathartic.

TO STUFF AND BAKE FISH.

Soak bread in cold water until soft; drain it, mash it fine, and mix the bread with a spoonful of drawn butter, a little salt and pepper (two raw eggs make the dressing cut smoother), and some spices if liked. Fill and sew up the fish; put a teacup of water in a bake pan, and a little butter; place in the fish and bake about forty or fifty minutes. Bass, shad and fresh cod are good fish for baking.

Hood's Sarsaparilla builds up the system while it eradicates disease.

STEWED OYSTERS.

Put one quart oysters and one-half pint water into a tin pail and set it into a kettle of boiling water; let it boil till the oysters are cooked, then strain, putting the oysters into a soup tureen and the liquor back into the pail, and add to it one pint milk, set in water as before, and heat boiling hot, seasoning with salt and pepper. Add to the oysters a piece of butter the size of an egg; lastly pour the hot liquor on the oysters.

LOBSTER SALAD.

Four eggs, one tablespoonful of sugar, two of butter, one of salt, two of vinegar, one of mustard; beat the whites of the eggs separately and add last. Cook in a bowl set in a kettle of water, stirring until it thickens. When cold add cream enough to make as thin as boiled custard. Add salt and red pepper to the chopped lobster and lettuce.

Invest 25 cents in a bottle of Hood's Tooth Powder.

STEWED LOBSTER.

Cut the lobster in pieces about an inch square. Place them in a stew pan, and over them pour a cup of water; put in butter the size of an egg, pepper and salt to the taste. Mix also with it the green dressing of the lobster, and stir it about ten minutes over the fire. Just before taking off add two wineglasses of port or sherry. Let it scald, but not boil.

True testimonials on another page as to Hood's Sarsaparilla,

Why Suffer with Salt Rheum?

MESSRS. C. I. HOOD & CO., Lowell, Mass.

Gentlemen:—I was a great sufferer from Salt Rheum on my limbs, for a dozen years previous to the summer of 1876, at which time I was cured by Hood's Sarsaparilla. The skin would become dry, chap, crack open, bleed and itch intensely, so that I could not help scratching, which of course made them worse. At the time I commenced taking Hood's Sarsaparilla (in the summer of 1876), they were so bad that they discharged, and I was obliged to keep them bandaged with linen cloths. The skin was drawn so tight by the heat of the disease that if I stooped over they would crack open and actually bring tears into my eyes. The first bottle benefited me so much that I continued taking it till I was cured. I used one box of Hood's Olive Ointment, to relieve the itching. Hoping many others may learn the value of Hood's Sarsaparilla and receive as much benefit as I have, I am, Very truly yours,

MRS. S. S. MOODY,

Lowell, Mass., January 15th, 1878. No. 75 Broadway.

FROM THE

"*Lowell Daily Citizen and News.*"

"The enterprising firm of Hood & Co. are doing a rushing business in HOOD'S SARSAPARILLA and HOOD'S TOOTH POWDER, both well known and appreciated by thousands who have tested their efficacy The Sarsaparilla has effected wonderful cures, not only in this city, but in various parts of New England, where its merits are as well known as here."

Hood's Tooth Powder is in everybody's mouth.

49

LOBSTER SAUCE.

Boil two eggs three minutes; mix with them a teaspoonful of water and the spawn of the lobster; rub smooth and stir in a teaspoonful of mustard, six spoonfuls of drawn butter or salad oil, a little pepper and salt, and five spoonfuls of vinegar. Cut the Lobster into very small pieces, and stew it till tender.

Hood's Sarsaparilla gives tone to the stomach.

PICKLED PEACHES.

One-half peck peaches, two pounds brown sugar, one ounce stick cinnamon, one pint vinegar. Boil sugar and vinegar together twenty minutes. Put peaches in hot water for an instant, and on taking them out rub the fur off with a coarse towel; now stick four cloves in each peach, then put them in the syrup and boil till tender.

SCALLOPED OYSTERS.

Sprinkle a buttered dish with bread or cracker crumbs, then put in a layer of oysters, some bits of butter, a little pepper and very little salt, and so on until the dish is full, leaving crumbs and butter on the top. Pour over the top a little wine. Bake until a light brown.

Hood's Tooth Powder gives the gums a bright, healthy color.

FRIED OYSTERS.

Select the largest, dip them in beaten egg, and then in bread or cracker crumbs; fry in equal parts of butter and lard until they are brown. They are very good dipped in corn meal instead of crumbs.

PICKLED OYSTERS.

One quart vinegar, one ounce of allspice, one-half ounce of cinnamon, one ounce of cloves, one ounce of mace; scald all together; when cold put in the oysters; next day scald together.

Now is the time to try Hood's Sarsaparilla.

CHICKEN SALAD.

Boil, bone and chop fine three chickens; use chopped celery; take equal quantities of meat and salad and mix with the following dressing: yolks of three eggs, stir them with a fork, then stir in slowly a cup of melted butter; do not put in faster than will mingle nicely. Salt to taste, and add a teaspoonful of powdered sugar, a cup of vinegar and a pinch of red pepper.

Hood's Sarsaparilla cures scrofulous humor.

SALAD CREAM DRESSING.

Two even tablespoonfuls dry mustard, one teaspoonful salt, one teaspoonful powdered sugar; scald with hot water enough to mix. Pour in the oil slowly, beating all the time, drop in all the oil it will contain, put in three unbeaten eggs and beat all together; now add one-half cup of vinegar and then two-thirds cup milk; put over the fire and bring to a boil, stirring constantly. Strain if you wish.

COFFEE.

The best coffee is made from Mocha and Java, mixed. To a pint of coffee add a gallon of water and three eggs.

Decorate your mouth with pearly teeth by using Hood's Tooth Powder.

MEAD.

Three pounds of white sugar; pour three pints of boiling water over it, one pint of molasses, one-fourth pound tartaric acid, one ounce of sassafras. To be bottled and used as a syrup with soda.

FLAX SEED TEA.

Put to two tablespoonfuls whole flax seed a pint of boiling water, and boil fifteen minutes; cut up one lemon and put in a pitcher with two tablespoonfuls of sugar. Strain the tea boiling hot through a wire strainer into the pitcher and stir together. Good for cough and sore throat.

BOILED CIDER.

Take four gallons of cider and boil it to one gallon.

SHAKER, OR BOILED CIDER APPLE SAUCE.

For one bushel of sweet apples use one gallon of boiled cider; put the cider into a brass or tin boiler, wash and drain the apples, then put them into the boiler and cover tight. If the boiler will hold one bushel of apples, two hours should be given for cooking. Care should be taken that they do not cling to the boiler or scorch; cook very slow over a moderate heat, but steady; do not stir them while cooking.

To remove all humors of the blood use Hood's Sarsaparilla.

HOOD'S RASPBERRY VINEGAR

Should be used at every picnic, in every sick room, and on every sideboard, *because* it quenches thirst at once. It forms with ice water a refreshing, healthful beverage, and its delicious flavor is especially appreciated by invalids. Physicians prescribe it. Prepared only by C. I. Hood & Co., opposite Postoffice, Lowell, Mass.

RIPE CUCUMBER PICKLE.

Take large yellow cucumbers, pare them, take out the cores and soak in salt water two days. Then take them out of the brine, pour over them boiling water, and let them stand over night. Pour off this water and they are ready for the pickle, which prepare thus: For each quart of sharp vinegar, take one pint of hot water, two large cups of sugar, and one tablespoonful each of the following spices: cinnamon, cloves, allspice, black pepper, mace or nutmeg. Add a handful of raisins or ripe grapes. Scald all together and boil until the cucumbers are easily penetrated with a fork. Use as little of the vinegar as possible to boil them in, and pour the rest over them when done.

SWEET PICKLE.

Seven pounds of fruit, two pounds of sugar, one quart of vinegar, two ounces of cassia buds or cloves.

THOSE PEOPLE

Who are suffering from scrofulous sores are specially requested to read Miss Whittier's testimonial on page 23 of Hood's Cook Book.

A FARMER IN VERMONT

Who had a *CANCER CUT OUT* some years ago, tells us that he can do double the work when he takes Hood's Sarsaparilla.

"EAT, SLEEP AND WORK."

A carpenter out of health and seriously troubled with blood-shot eyes and inflamed lids, tells us: "Hood's Sarsaparilla has done everything for me; can eat, sleep and work now, and my eyes are nearly well."

Hood's Sarsaparilla is prepared only by

C. I. HOOD & CO., Apothecaries,

LOWELL, MASS.

Trial Size, 50 cents; large bottles, $1.00.

Hood's Tooth Powder whitens the teeth.

GREEN CUCUMBER PICKLES.

For a half bushel cucumbers, take a pint of coarse salt, dissolve in water enough to cover the cucumbers, pour it boiling hot upon them, let them stand twenty-four hours, pour the brine off, and reheat two successive mornings. The fourth morning drain off the brine, and pour on boiling water; let them stand twenty-four hours, then if the cucumbers are not filled out plump, pour in boiling water again. When the cucumbers are all filled out plump they are ready for the vinegar. Place them in the jar in which they are to be kept, and as they are packed place in little bags containing whole allspice, cloves, cinnamon and mustard. Put a little horse-radish root among the cucumbers. Heat vinegar enough to cover the cucumbers, with a piece of alum dissolved in it, pour it over them boiling hot. Cover tight.

Hood's Sarsaparilla imparts new life to all the functions of the body.

SPICED CURRANTS.

Seven pounds currants, four pounds sugar, one pint vinegar (if of average strength), one tablespoonful of cinnamon, one tablespoonful of cloves, one teaspoonful allspice. Give it two hours or more slow boiling.

PICKLED APPLES.

One quart vinegar, six cups brown sugar, one teaspoonful each of cloves, cinnamon, allspice; boil vinegar and sugar together, skim it, then add the spices. Boil in this syrup sweet apples cut in halves and not pared, till soft, but not till they break.

TOMATO KETCHUP.

Eight quarts of strained tomato, six tablespoonfuls of black pepper, six tablespoonfuls of salt, four tablespoonfuls mustard, one tablespoonful ground cloves, one tablespoonful yellow ginger, one quart vinegar, one-half cup of brown sugar, one tumbler of brandy. Boil very slowly until the quantity is reduced nearly one-half. Put into bottles.

The proprietors of Hood's Sarsaparilla take great pleasure in hearing of the remarkable cures effected by the use of their Sarsaparilla. Yesterday we were told of a young lady who had been a great sufferer for several years with a *TERRIBLE SCROFULOUS SORE ON HER LEG.* Six bottles Hood's Sarsaparilla has entirely cured it; and any one having a similar affliction can appreciate how happy she is now. An elderly lady who has been and is still a great sufferer from one of these awful scrofulous sores or ulcers on her leg, which seems more like a cancer than anything, tells us that she has used half a bottle—in one-half teaspoonful doses—her general health is very much better, the discharge from her sore has not been so offensive since the first week after taking Hood's Sarsaparilla; sleeps better nights; her food does not distress her as before, and when the sore bleeds the blood has a bright, healthy color, and before it was very black and thick.

Hood's Sarsaparilla is prepared only by

C. I. HOOD & CO., - - Apothecaries,

LOWELL, MASS.

Trial size, 50 cents; large bottles, $1.00.

Hood's Tooth Powder is delightful to use.

55

TOMATO CHOW CHOW.

Slice one peck green tomatoes, six green peppers, four onions; stir in a cup of salt and let them remain over night. Then pour off the water, put them in a kettle with vinegar enough to cover them. Add one cup of grated horse-radish, one tablespoonful of cloves, one tablespoonful of cinnamon, one tablespoonful of allspice, one cup of sugar; cook until soft.

Scrofula and salt rheum have been cured by Hood's Sarsaparilla.

TOMATO PICKLE.

One gallon sliced tomatoes, the greener the better; salt them in layers, and let them stand over night; in the morning drain them well; slice four large onions; put a layer of tomatoes in the vessel, then a few slices of onion; proceed in this manner until they are all put in; cut six green peppers very fine and spread over the top; take one tablespoonful black pepper, one tablespoonful allspice, two tablespoonfuls of cloves, three tablespoonfuls mustard; put in a bag and boil in the vinegar till the strength is extracted, then put the bag on the top of the pickles, pour on boiling vinegar enough to cover them. Cover the vessel tightly and let it stand three weeks without opening.

CITRON PICKLE.

Pare and cut citron into such pieces as you like; boil in water with a very small piece of alum, until tender, then drain; boil together for ten minutes three quarts of vinegar, four pounds of sugar and one-fourth pound of cassia buds; put in the citron and boil five minutes.

Hood's Tooth Powder is praised by everybody.

CHILI SAUCE.

Six large, ripe tomatoes, four green peppers, one onion, one tablespoonful of sugar, one tablespoonful of salt, one and a half cups strong vinegar; chop peppers and onions; boil one hour.

Hood's Sarsaparilla sharpens the appetite.

MESSRS. C. I. HOOD & CO., Lowell.

CHELSEA, VT., Sept., 1877.

Dear Sirs:—I have used Hood's Saponaceous Tooth Powder in my practice for several years and can assure the public that it is an article worthy their entire confidence. It combines all the materials requisite for a safe and efficacious dentifrice, put together in such a manner as to cleanse the teeth thoroughly, harden the gums, and give them a bright color, and its delightful fragrance leaves a peculiar, refreshing sweetness in the mouth.

Respectfully yours,

O. M. RICE, DENTIST.

SCIENTIFIC EXAMINATIONS PROVE

Hood's Saponaceous Tooth Powder

The most effectual in destroying the animal and vegetable parasitic animalculæ, which are the cause of decay and are found to exist on nearly all teeth.

HOOD'S TOOTH POWDER is so happily put up as to offer to every one the means for cleansing, beautifying and preserving their teeth and gums, at small expense. The peculiar sweetness it imparts to the breath, and the delightful cool sensation it leaves in the mouth, render its use exceedingly pleasant. The assurances of its entirely harmless nature, which we give from eminent men, should be sufficient to satisfy any reasonable mind.

HOOD'S TOOTH POWDER receives the sanction and patronage of the most eminent of the dental and medical faculty.

HOOD'S TOOTH POWDER should be used by every man, woman and child, for good health depends upon cleanliness, and where is its necessity more apparent than in the mouth?

HOOD'S TOOTH POWDER is sold everywhere in large bottles at 25 cents.

PREPARED ONLY BY

C. I. HOOD & CO., = = *Apothecaries,*

LOWELL, MASS.

CLARA'S CORN CAKE—NICE.

Butter size of an egg, tablespoonful sugar, two eggs, beat to a cream; not quite a quart of milk; flour to make as thick as sponge cake, then add a large handful of Indian meal; two teaspoonfuls yeast powder in the flour before mixing.

IMPERIAL CAKE.

One pound sugar, one pound butter, one pound flour, one pound raisins, one-half pound almonds, one-half pound citron, very little soda, eight eggs, mace to taste, wineglass of wine.

FRUIT CAKE—EXTRA.

One pound butter, one pound sugar, one pound flour, two pounds currants, two pounds raisins, one-half pound citron, eight eggs, one-half cup molasses, soda size of pea dissolved in molasses, mace, nutmeg, cinnamon and cloves to suit taste, wineglass of brandy.

HEARTS AND ROUNDS.

One cup butter, two cups sugar, one cup milk, three cups flour, five eggs, two even teaspoonfuls cream tartar, one even teaspoonful soda, citron. Flavor with lemon or vanilla.

RIBBON CAKE.

Two cups of sugar, three eggs, two-thirds of a cup of butter, one cup of sweet milk, three cups of flour, one teaspoonful of saleratus dissolved in the milk, add a little salt and flavor with essence of lemon or almond. Put half the above in two square oblong pans. To the remainder add one tablespoonful of molasses, one large cup of raisins stoned and chopped, a quarter of a pound of citron sliced, one teaspoonful cinnamon, half a teaspoonful each clove and allspice, grate in a little nutmeg and add one spoonful of flour. Put into two pans of the same size and shape as those above. Put the sheets together while warm, alternately, with a little jelly or raspberry jam between. Cut in thin slices for the table. It will cut most easily the day after it is baked. It may be baked in one large pan without the fruit, pouring in the dark and light in alternate layers. When baked thus it is a handsome marble cake.

A lady having a *CANCEROUS HUMOR IN THE STOMACH* is using Hood's Sarsaparilla, and tells us she is very much encouraged, and thinks it is doing her a great deal of good. She is now taking the second bottle. A young lady who had been a great sufferer from *PAIN IN THE BONES* of her arm and shoulder and through her lungs, her general health very poor, no appetite, and her friends feared she was going into a decline, as her family have died of consumption, has taken nearly two bottles Hood's Sarsaparilla; has no pain now, has a good appetite and is steadily improving.

We could add to these, remarkable as they may seem, almost an infinite number, if we would note them down as one after another, in their gratitude for the relief and benefit received, tell us their story.

Hood's Sarsaparilla is prepared only by

C. I. HOOD & CO., Apothecaries,

LOWELL, MASS.

Trial size, 50 cents; large bottles, $1.00.

Hood's Sarsaparilla restores flesh; see page 25.

What Lowell Dentists say of
Hood's Tooth Powder.

LOWELL, MASS., Jan. 18, 1878.

Gentlemen :—We have made a critical examination of Hood's Saponaceous Tooth Powder, and can assure the public that it does not contain anything that can possibly injure the teeth, either mechanically or chemically.

Very truly yours,

G. A. GERRY, Five Cent Savings Bank Block.

A. T. JOHNSON, Wentworth's Block.

G. A. W. VINAL, Wentworth's Block.

C. T. CLIFFORD, Stott's Block.

W. H. DOWNS, Fiske's Block.

B. HEALD, 52½ Merrimack Street.

E. M. NELSON, 84 Merrimack Street.

To Messrs. C. I. HOOD & Co., Lowell, Mass.

Hands that Crack Open and Bleed Cured.

A few days since a lady, while buying her third bottle of Hood's Sarsaparilla, remarked: "Without any expectation that your Sarsaparilla would help my hands, from which I have suffered exceedingly for many years, of Salt Rheum, which would cause them to itch terribly, dry up, finally crack open and bleed, I bought a bottle at the earnest solicitation of my husband, who had known of Mrs. Moody's wonderful cure. (See page 48.) You can hardly imagine my delight when they began to heal. Before I commenced the second bottle they were entirely well, and have not troubled me since. I shall continue to take it till I have used six bottles, for I want to purify my blood thoroughly, and I have an immense amount of faith in Hood's Sarsaparilla now, and with good reason."

Hood's Tooth Powder removes tartar from the teeth.

TWO GOOD REASONS WHY

You should gladly send a testimonial of the benefits you have received from the use of Hood's Sarsaparilla to C. I. Hood & Co., Lowell, Mass.

First, because it is a duty you owe to others who are now suffering as you were before you found relief in this valuable remedy.

Second, because there are so many worthless remedies puffed up by bogus certificates, that the fact that there is one of real worth is of great importance to the public.

---

135 Howard St., LOWELL, MASS., Jan. 17, 1878.

MESSRS. C. I. HOOD & CO.

Gentlemen:—I have used Hood's Sarsaparilla in my family for Scrofulous Humor with wonderful success and am very happy to tell you that it is the best medicine we ever used. I do sincerely advise any one who is troubled with Scrofula to give this valuable remedy a trial and assure them they will not be disappointed.

Very truly yours,

(Coburn Shuttle Co.)   C. C. PICKERING.

Pimples on the Face Removed.

Mt. Washington St., Jan. 17th, 1878.

GENTLEMEN:—

Last summer I got a bottle of Hood's Sarsaparilla for my son, who has been very much troubled with pimples on his face, which came to a white fester on the top. While using this bottle they came freer, but before he had finished it they entirely disappeared and have not returned. I cheerfully recommend Hood's Sarsaparilla as a reliable medicine.

Very truly yours,

ALEXANDER ANDERSON.

NOTICE.—If you have Hood's Cook Book, please give this to your neighbor.

INDEX.

Hood's Tooth Powder, the cheapest and best.

Ladies, remember that Hood's Sarsaparilla vitalizes and enriches the blood.

What leading Dentists say of Hood's Tooth Powder.

The following from Dr. Gerry, one of our leading dentists, a graduate of the Boston Dental College, with twenty-five years of practical experience, is worthy of consideration:

LOWELL, MASS., Sept. 25, 1877.

Gentlemen:—I have made a critical examination of Hood's Saponaceous Tooth Powder, and can assure the public that it does not contain anything that can possibly injure the teeth, either mechanically or chemically.

Very truly yours,

G. A. GERRY, D. D. S.

To Messrs. C. I. Hood & Co., Lowell, Mass.

One of the most successful dentists in Boston writes us as follows:

BOSTON, MASS., Oct. 15, 1877.

MESSRS. C. I. HOOD & CO., Lowell, Mass.

My Dear Sirs:—I have used Hood's Tooth Powder in my family and recommended it to my patients for several years with excellent satisfaction to them and to myself. As a preserver and cleanser of the teeth it can not be surpassed. My knowledge of the materials of which it is made enables me to assure the public that it is impossible for it to do any injury to the teeth or gums. It affords me much pleasure in commending it to all as a safe and effective dentifrice.

Very truly yours,

THOMAS COGSWELL, D. D. S.,
Lawrence's Building, Tremont Street.

This letter from Dr. Gerrish affords us much satisfaction, and will inspire in the minds of all who have the pleasure of his acquaintance perfect confidence in Hood's Tooth Powder:

EXETER, N. H., September, 1877.

MESSRS. C. I. HOOD & CO., Lowell.

Gentlemen:—It gives me much pleasure to commend Hood's Saponaceous Tooth Powder to the public. In my profession it has worked like a charm; in my family and among my friends it has proved itself satisfactory in the highest possible degree. Delightful to use and so efficacious in cleansing the teeth and hardening the gums that I predict for you a sale that will rapidly increase as its real worth becomes more generally known.

Very truly,

CHARLES H. GERRISH, D. D. S.

Every one having humors should try Hood's Sarsaparilla.

Hood's Sarsaparilla

CURES SCROFULA,
CURES SCROFULOUS HUMOR.
CURES SALT-RHEUM,
CURES CANCEROUS HUMOR.
CURES SCALD HEAD.
CURES BOILS.

CURES SYPHILITIC AFFECTIONS,
CURES PAIN IN THE BONES,
CURES GENERAL DEBILITY,
CURES FEMALE WEAKNESSES,
CURES COSTIVENESS,
CURES HEADACHE.

Hood's Sarsaparilla purifies the Blood of all Humors.

Hood's Sarsaparilla vitalizes and enriches the Blood.

Hood's Sarsaparilla restores and renovates the whole system.

Hood's Sarsaparilla stimulates and invigorates all the functions of the body.

A peculiar point in Hood's Sarsaparilla is that it strengthens and builds up the system, while it eradicates disease, and as Nature's great assistant proves itself invaluable as a protection from diseases that originate in changes of the seasons, of climate and of life.

———◦◦———

PREPARED ONLY BY

C. I. HOOD & CO., Apothecaries,

Barristers' Hall, Lowell, Mass.

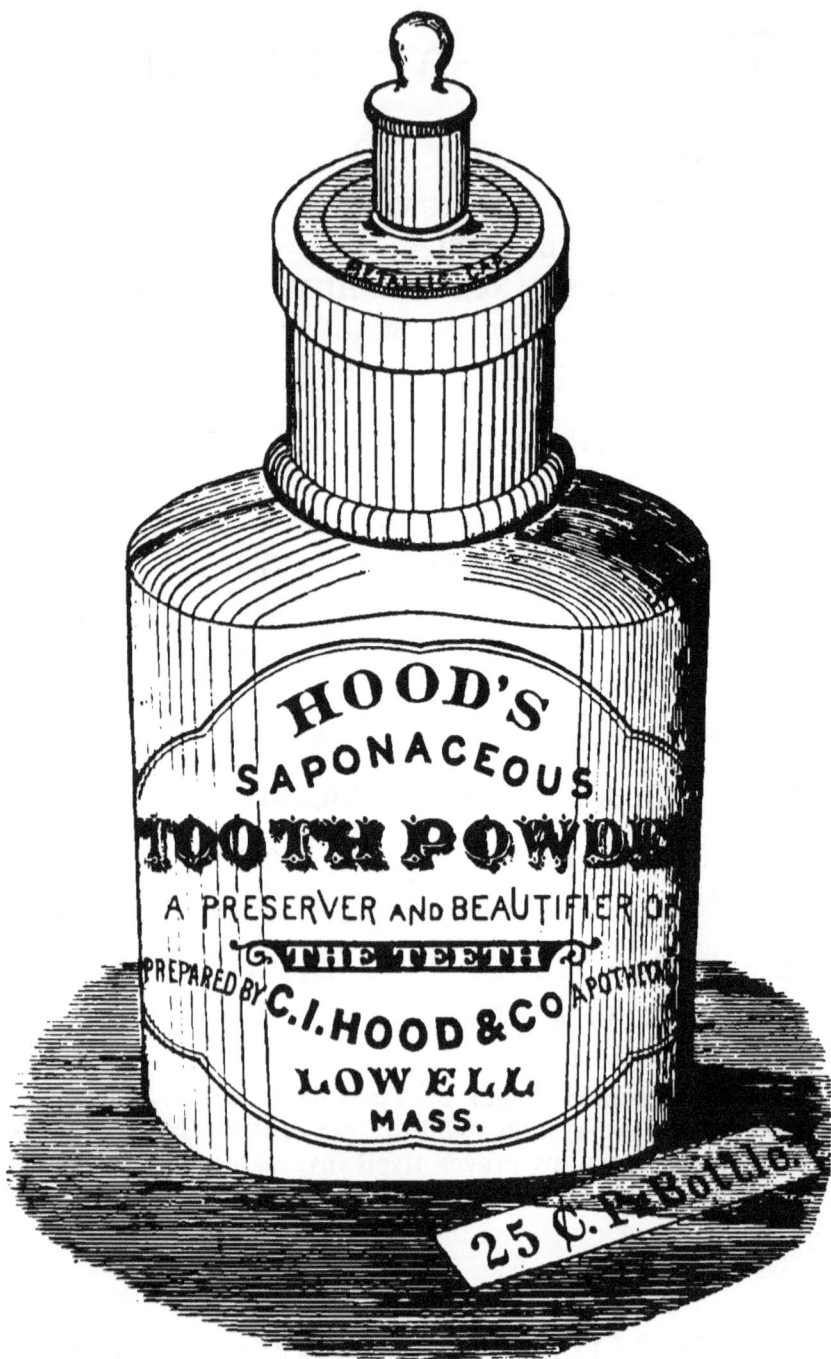

www.ingramcontent.com/pod-product-compliance
Lightning Source LLC
Chambersburg PA
CBHW021517090426
42739CB00007B/650